JOURNAL
THERAPY
~ *for* ~
# CALMING
# ANXIETY

366 Prompts to
Help Reduce Stress and
Create Inner Peace

~

KATHLEEN ADAMS, LPC
Registered Poetry/Journal Therapist

STERLING
New York

STERLING
New York

An Imprint of Sterling Publishing Co., Inc.
122 Fifth Avenue
New York, NY 10011

ISBN 978-1-4549-4013-5

Distributed in Canada by Sterling Publishing Co., Inc.
c/o Canadian Manda Group, 664 Annette Street
Toronto, Ontario M6S 2C8, Canada
Distributed in the United Kingdom by GMC Distribution Services
Castle Place, 166 High Street, Lewes, East Sussex BN7 1XU, England
Distributed in Australia by NewSouth Books
University of New South Wales, Sydney, NSW 2052, Australia

For information about custom editions, special sales, and premium and corporate purchases,
please contact Sterling Special Sales at 800-805-5489 or specialsales@sterlingpublishing.com.

Manufactured in Canada

2 4 6 8 10 9 7 5 3 1

www.sterlingpublishing.com

Cover design by David Ter-Avanesyan
Interior design by Gina Bonanno

Cover image by Login/Shutterstock.com
Interior art by Shutterstock: Binkski: Week 29–32;
Anteya Damaskina: Week 1–4, Week 33–36;
Forgem: Week 21–24; Fire Irbis: Week 49–52, Week 17–20;
Mikhail Prokhorov: Week 13–16, Week 45–48;
SaveJungle: Week 5–8, Week 37–40;
Vertyr: Week 24–28; Wikki: Week 9–12;

Dedicated to my sister,
Susan J. Phillips, EdD,
my first and always teacher

INTRODUCTION

A staggering 40 million American adults struggle with anxiety, according to the Anxiety and Depression Association of America. Of these, only 37 percent receive treatment, so there are at least 25 million folks who bravely lean on family, friends, and self-help for support.

The origins of anxiety can be complex and may be attributable to a stew of genetics, brain chemistry, personality, trauma, or life events. Generally, though, it's not that useful to explore the "why" of anxiety. It's usually more productive to focus on the here and now, developing new skills to support cognitive, behavioral, emotional, and neurological change.

But change can be hard, and it takes time.

Here's the good news for those who suffer from anxiety: You can shift your thinking and feeling, perhaps dramatically, in one year. You might even start seeing benefits in as little as two months. The secret? *Intention* (your own desire and determination), *attention* (the deliberate focus on training your mind, body, and emotions), and *action* (regular writing and concomitant behavioral change).

With consistent practice, the benefits tend to amplify. The kindling fire at two months is a steadily burning log after a year.

Here's more good news: Well-being is a skill that can be learned. The research of neuropsychologist Dr. Richard Davidson validates this. He, along with many of his colleagues in the emerging science of neuroplasticity, is finding that *mindfulness* is a big factor in the capacity of the brain to change itself in positive ways.

Dr. Jon Kabat-Zinn defines *mindfulness* as "paying attention in a particular way: on purpose, in the present moment, and nonjudgmentally." Typically the development of mindfulness is associated with meditation, which helps cultivate a certain attitude of curiosity, kindness, and the acceptance of the mind's present-moment thought process and experience.

Meditation, though, is not the only path to mindfulness. The work of Washington, DC–based psychotherapist and journal therapist Deborah Ross, founder of the *Your Brain on Ink* method of self-directed neuroplasticity, suggests that writing in a journal in an intentional way can be similarly powerful, particularly when enhanced by simultaneously practicing mindfulness in everyday life.

I've been writing in a journal since I was 10 years old, and I've devoted my professional life to following "the way of the journal" since 1985. I taught my first journal workshop (then called Write On!) to six friends that autumn. I was a first-semester counseling graduate student, and I knew immediately that the intersection of writing and healing would be my life's work.

Along the way, I have learned the myriad ways writing can reach in and find the places that are stuck, the places that need soothing, or the places we want to explore but find locked doors. In her book *A Walk Between Heaven and Earth,* Burghild Nina Holzer writes, "Talking to paper is talking to the divine. It is talking to an ear that will understand even the most difficult things. Paper is infinitely patient."

I define *journal therapy* as the purposeful and intentional use of life-based writing as a tool for healing, growth, and change. In my 35-year career as a pioneer in the field, I have worked with tens of thousands of people to create writing routes to healthier, happier lives. This book incorporates my best practices in both journal therapy and the treatment of anxiety.

Well-being is a skill that can be learned. Journal writing is a process that supports well-being. This book, when completed sequentially over 12 months or more, can shift your relationship with anxiety through a step-by-step process to create or strengthen better-feeling thoughts and an active engagement with your own well-being.

—Kathleen Adams, LPC
Registered Poetry/Journal Therapist

How to Gain the Most from This Journal

This journal offers a yearlong study of anxiety management strategies, cognitive-behavioral techniques, neuroscience principles, mindfulness approaches, and journal therapy best practices. For best results:

☀ Work at your own pace. You do not need to write every day. You'll have the best outcomes if you write sequentially to each prompt, even if you have days between entries.

☀ Plan to spend about 5 to 10 minutes per prompt. If you want to write more or less, feel free. Save a minute or two at the end of each entry to read through your writing and harvest your insights in a reflection write (Week 1, Day 2).

☀ Skip any prompt that you feel isn't relevant or is overly provocative. Expressive writing researcher Dr. James Pennebaker's "Flip-Out Rule" offers a guideline: "If you think you're about to flip out, stop writing." (Week 3, Day 6)

☀ Write in an outside journal dedicated to this process. It can be a notebook, blank book, digital app, or computer file. It will be helpful to date your pages and include the week/day numbers for cross-referencing.

☀ There is no significant difference in outcomes between writing by hand and writing by keyboard, so long as you are comfortable with the method you're using. Do what feels easiest or most natural to you.

Most of the days from week to week include a variety of activities. The first day of each week has been reserved for setting your intentions for that week. The fourth day of each week covers the repeating theme of Dr. Davidson's four keys to well-being. These compile over time, offering you opportunities to self-chart and track your own development. The seventh day is a review of the week. The prompts themselves fall into several categories. These include:

- Weekly intention setting (Day 1)

- Four keys to well-being (neuroscience) (Day 4)

- Weekly review (Day 7)

- Write on! (journal techniques, tips, and best practices)

- Science (research studies and practices drawn from experts)

- Survey (anxiety management strategies shared with permission from a survey of nearly 200 people with anxiety, some of whom you will meet by first name)

- Strategies (tips, techniques, and applications in many subject areas)

In the course of this exploration, you may come to a realization that your anxiety management would benefit from outside support. Please seek professional help if needed.

The late poet Richard Solly once said that writing in a journal takes courage and sweaters. Congratulations on your courage in undertaking a program that hopefully will offer you opportunities for growth and positive change. Along the way, wrap yourself in sweaters of self-care and self-discovery. Write on!

A TINY STORY. Let's start with you. What's your life like right now? Set your timer for three minutes and then wrap up. Don't worry about spelling or anything else. Just write.

WRITE ON! Write a tiny story about your life. Who's in it? How do you spend your time? Where is home? Bullet lists are fine, as are fragments or random bursts of thought.

REFLECTION. This is a key tool in the journal toolbox. After you've written, read over, and then write a sentence or two of feedback. "As I read this, I notice . . ." or, "I'm surprised by . . ." or, "I'm curious about . . ." The reflection write harvests insight. It is the express elevator to clarity.

WRITE ON! Read over your Day 1 writing. Then tell yourself what just happened. What surprised you? What do you notice?

_____

_____

_____

_____

_____

_____

INTENTION, ATTENTION, ACTION. Journal therapist and author of _Your Brain on Ink_ Deborah Ross suggests this trilogy to align your act of writing with neurological principles. First, center yourself and set an _intention_ for your writing. Then place your _attention_ on the prompt or technique and take _action_ by writing from a thoughtful, mindful space.

WRITE ON! Try it! Center yourself. Set an intention. Place your attention. When you're ready, write. Read and reflect.

_____

_____

_____

_____

_____

_____

See the Introduction for a discussion on the work of Dr. Richard Davidson, with the core message that well-being is a skill that can be learned.

KEY #1: RESILIENCE. The first of Dr. Davidson's four keys to well-being is resilience. We begin here even though resilience is the key that is most difficult to master. Its development is reliant on how well your brain recovers from adverse events. Resilience requires that you fall down a lot and build skills to get back up.

WRITE ON! Write your own story of resilience in 5 to 10 minutes. Read back and write a reflection.

_____

_____

_____

_____

_____

_____

_____

_____

_____

_____

_____

_____

_____

_____

_____

_____

_____

_____

_____

ANXIETY'S STORY. Anxiety has been your companion for some time. How did it come to you? How old were you? What was the first hint of trouble? How has it progressed?

WRITE ON! Set your timer for five minutes. Write for more or less time, as you wish. What is Anxiety's story? Read and reflect. Did you encounter any surprises or insights?

RAYS OF LIGHT. No matter how challenging things may be, there's always at least one thing that's going well. It might be a relationship that you can count on, a cause that fills you with purpose, a pastime that sparks your imagination. What is one ray of light today?

WRITE ON! Write about a ray of light that is shining on you right now. Start with five minutes, and write more if you want. Read back and reflect.

_____

_____

_____

_____

_____

_____

_____

WEEKLY REVIEW. Read over the week's entries, reflections, or both. How do you rank your anxiety this week? How do you rank your use of writing?

On a scale of 1 (low) to 7 (high), rate your week:

Anxiety?	①	②	③	④	⑤	⑥	⑦
Writing process?	①	②	③	④	⑤	⑥	⑦
Noticing shifts?	①	②	③	④	⑤	⑥	⑦

WRITE ON! Write observations as you rate your week. Note any connections you may see.

_____

_____

_____

_____

_____

_____

INTENTION VS. GOAL. Intentions and goals are outcomes we envision and move toward. While goals are often externally driven, intentions tend to be internally sourced. In this journal you'll write intentions on the first day of your week. If you prefer to call them goals, please do.

WRITE ON! What is your intention for this 12-month journal (knowing it might take longer than a year to complete)? What do you want to do, be, or have at the end of the process?

_____

_____

_____

_____

_____

_____

_____

_____

_____

_____

_____

_____

_____

_____

_____

_____

_____

_____

_____

_____

_____

_____

PRIVATE! KEEP OUT! Your journal is your private book or digital file. No one has the right to read it without your permission. If your family respects boundaries, tell them you're writing an anxiety journal and ask for their support by not snooping. If that won't work, try a digital journal in the cloud, a password-protected app, obscurely named folders, or a flash drive. In a paper journal, write **PRIVATE! KEEP OUT!** on the cover and first page. Stash it in your book bag, backpack, or locking file drawer.

WRITE ON! How will you protect your privacy? Write and reflect.

_____

_____

_____

_____

_____

_____

MINDFULNESS PANTRY. Mindfulness skill development includes attention to self-care such as healthy nutrition, sufficient quality sleep, adequate hydration, conscious breathwork, experiences in nature, exercise, creating quality relationships, connection with meaning (religion, tradition, spirituality, core values), self-regulation, appreciating beauty, and shifting to better-feeling thoughts—all with education and practice.

WRITE ON! Imagine that you can store these skills, and others, in a large kitchen. What's in your pantry? What's missing?

_____

_____

_____

_____

_____

_____

KEY #2: OUTLOOK. The second of Dr. Davidson's four keys to well-being is outlook: What's your worldview? Can you find the lessons in even hard situations? Do you see others as essentially good human beings? He stresses compassion and kindness, reporting that the start of neurological change happens "quite quickly, after a very, very modest dose of practice."

WRITE ON! What is your outlook? Write for 5 to 10 minutes. Then read and reflect.

_____

_____

_____

_____

_____

_____

_____

_____

_____

_____

_____

_____

_____

_____

_____

_____

_____

_____

_____

_____

_____

RELAXATION RESPONSE. Cardiologist Herbert Benson developed the Relaxation Response in 1976, sourced in his desire to help heart patients get healthier. It has become a mindfulness resource for millions.

WRITE ON! Choose a focus word (Dr. Benson recommends "one"). Internally repeat your word on the exhale of deep breaths. Progressively relax your body from your toes up. Passively disregard thoughts; internally say, "oh well," and return to your breath. Write for five minutes and reflect.

PRACTICE: RELAXATION RESPONSE. Throughout this journal you'll find that we sometimes return to earlier prompts. This cues your brain to pay attention and deepen the experience. Sometimes these are to practice and sometimes to touch back and extend.

WRITE ON! Practice yesterday's Relaxation Response again. What do you notice?

_____

_____

_____

_____

_____

_____

_____

WEEKLY REVIEW. Read over the week's entries, reflections, or both. How do you rank your anxiety this week? How do you rank your use of writing? How is the realistic progress of your intentions going? Are you noticing changes?

On a scale of 1 (low) to 7 (high), rate your week:

Anxiety?	①	②	③	④	⑤	⑥	⑦
Writing process?	①	②	③	④	⑤	⑥	⑦
Intentions?	①	②	③	④	⑤	⑥	⑦
Noticing shifts?	①	②	③	④	⑤	⑥	⑦

WRITE ON! Write observations as you rate your week. Note any connections you may see.

_____

_____

_____

_____

_____

SETTING INTENTION. Intentions are goals that are internally sourced. We want them not only for what they represent (a met deadline, a completed project, a shift in thinking or feeling) but also for how we'll feel (content, satisfied, regulated) as we move toward them.

WRITE ON! What are three intentions for this week? These can be related to any area of your life. Break larger intentions into week-size bites.

_____

_____

_____

_____

_____

_____

_____

FIVE-MINUTE SPRINT. Last week, you were guided to write five-minute sprints. Here's why: Five minutes is an accessible unit of time. You can hold focus for five minutes. Five minutes can yield a surprising amount of information and insight.

WRITE ON! Close your eyes and check in with your body. What are you feeling? Where do you feel it? Set your timer for five minutes. What do you notice?

_____

_____

_____

_____

_____

_____

_____

TOUCHBACK: RAYS OF LIGHT. In Week 1 you wrote about rays of light, areas of your life that are consistent anchors of goodness.

WRITE ON! Which ray of light is in the foreground for you today? Who or what is anchoring you? Write for 5 to 10 minutes. Read back and write a reflection.

_____

_____

_____

_____

_____

_____

_____

_____

_____

_____

_____

_____

_____

_____

_____

_____

_____

_____

_____

_____

_____

_____

_____

KEY #3: ATTENTION. The third key to well-being is attention. Attention is mindfulness in action. Attention keeps you in the present moment. It helps you focus. It helps you process. It supports clear, cohesive thinking.

WRITE ON! Write a list of three to five times in the past week when you have been fully present and paid attention, however briefly. Include sensory details. Then read and reflect. What do you notice?

_____

_____

_____

_____

_____

_____

_____

_____

_____

_____

_____

_____

_____

_____

_____

_____

_____

_____

_____

_____

5-4-3-2-1. Trauma and anxiety therapists recommend this simple but effective sensory grounding process. First, take deep breaths. Then, sequentially, name five things you see, four things you can touch, three things you hear, two things you smell, and one thing you taste.

WRITE ON! Write each sensory experience as a line in a "list poem." ("Now I am seeing . . ." "Now I am seeing . . ." "Now I am touching . . .") This deepens the experience and stores it in memory.

THE FLIP-OUT RULE. Dr. James Pennebaker is the primary researcher in the expressive writing field. You'll learn his writing model as we go along. One of Dr. Pennebaker's axioms is the Flip-Out Rule: "If you start to flip out, stop writing."

WRITE ON! We'll be covering a lot of topics, and some of them might feel difficult. You can always skip any prompt you don't like or feel comfortable with. For safety, can you agree to the Flip-Out Rule? What are your flip-out signals? Write them.

_____

_____

_____

_____

_____

_____

WEEKLY REVIEW. Read over the week's entries, reflections, or both. How do you rank your anxiety this week? How do you rank your use of writing? How is the realistic progress of your intentions going? Are you noticing changes?

On a scale of 1 (low) to 7 (high), rate your week:

Anxiety	①	②	③	④	⑤	⑥	⑦
Writing process?	①	②	③	④	⑤	⑥	⑦
Intentions?	①	②	③	④	⑤	⑥	⑦
Noticing shifts?	①	②	③	④	⑤	⑥	⑦

WRITE ON! Write observations as you rate your week. Note any connections you may see.

_____

_____

_____

_____

_____

SETTING INTENTION. Intentions are goals that are internally sourced. We want them not only for what they represent (a met deadline, a completed project, a shift in thinking or feeling) but also for how we'll feel (content, satisfied, regulated) as we move toward them.

WRITE ON! What are three intentions for this week? Remember to keep them week-size. Also, start checking in with last week's intentions. Carry over any that weren't completed.

_____

_____

_____

_____

_____

_____

LIST POEMS. List poems are just what they sound like—poems that take the form of a list. List poems feature interesting juxtapositions and the poetic device of repetition.

WRITE ON! A well-known list poem is George Ella Lyon's "Where I'm From." Do an Internet search for the poem along with a template to help construct your own "Where I'm From" poem.

_____

_____

_____

_____

_____

_____

_____

TOUCHBACK: ANXIETY'S PRAISEWORTHY CORE. Let's touch back to anxiety's origin story in Week 1. At the core of nearly everything, there is something worthy of praise. How has anxiety served you? What has it taught you?

WRITE ON! Write for five to seven minutes about anxiety's praiseworthy core. When you are finished, read back and write a reflection.

_____

_____

_____

_____

_____

_____

_____

_____

_____

_____

_____

_____

_____

_____

_____

_____

_____

_____

_____

_____

_____

KEY #4: GENEROSITY. Dr. Davidson states that there is "a plethora of data showing that when individuals engage in generous and altruistic behavior, they actually activate circuits in the brain that are key to fostering well-being." Generosity can be extended to the self as well as to others.

WRITE ON! What's your generosity style? How are you generous, and to whom? Are you generous to yourself?

_____

_____

_____

_____

_____

_____

_____

_____

_____

_____

_____

_____

_____

_____

_____

_____

_____

_____

_____

_____

WHY HYDRATION MATTERS. Prevailing medical advice is that we should drink around 64 ounces, or two quarts, of water a day, but lots of us don't follow that. Here's a good reason to hydrate: Scientists say dehydration and anxiety have similar physical symptoms, including feeling faint, light-headed, dizzy, agitated, foggy, and fatigued. Are you anxious—or thirsty?

WRITE ON! Write about your water intake. Create a strategy for sneaking in a few more glasses each day. Hydrate all week!

_____

_____

_____

_____

_____

_____

_____

_____

_____

_____

_____

_____

_____

_____

_____

_____

_____

_____

_____

TOUCHING WATER. Survey respondent Terri has a particular sensory experience with water. Some of her most reliable touchstones are to "get outside and touch a plant, even if it's raining, drink water, splash water on my face, wash my hands."

WRITE ON! How are you doing with hydration? Are you drinking more water? Pour yourself a tall cool glass and write a story about a positive experience of touching water.

_____

_____

_____

_____

_____

_____

WEEKLY REVIEW. Read over the week's entries, reflections, or both. How do you rank your anxiety this week? How do you rank your use of writing? How is the realistic progress of your intentions going? Are you noticing changes?

On a scale of 1 (low) to 7 (high), rate your week:

Anxiety	(1)	(2)	(3)	(4)	(5)	(6)	(7)
Writing process?	(1)	(2)	(3)	(4)	(5)	(6)	(7)
Intentions?	(1)	(2)	(3)	(4)	(5)	(6)	(7)
Noticing shifts?	(1)	(2)	(3)	(4)	(5)	(6)	(7)

WRITE ON! Write observations as you rate your week. Note any connections you may see.

_____

_____

_____

_____

_____

SETTING INTENTION. Intentions are goals that are internally sourced. We want them not only for what they represent (a met deadline, a completed project, a shift in thinking or feeling) but also for how we'll feel (content, satisfied, regulated) as we move toward them.

WRITE ON! What are three intentions for this week? You can set intentions for any area of your life. Check in with last week. Did you meet your intentions?

_____

_____

_____

_____

_____

_____

_____

_____

SENTENCE STEMS. Sometimes even a five-minute sprint is too much. That's when we bust out sentence stems. Start a sentence and let yourself complete it one or many times. Work quickly to encourage spontaneity.

WRITE ON! Make a list of sentence stems. "I want . . ." "The most important thing is . . ." "Anxiety is . . ." You get the idea. Write three more of your own. Finish your own sentence stems, one way or several ways each. Reflect.

_____

_____

_____

_____

_____

_____

_____

_____

THE "RULES." Your journal doesn't care if your writing is sloppy. If you can't spell, that's okay. You don't have to be a "good writer" or write every day. You can write by hand or on a keyboard. If there is a rule, it's this: Protect your privacy. (Also: the Flip-Out Rule from Week 3.)

WRITE ON! Are there rules about journal writing that inhibit you? Write them down. Can you release them? Scribble over those rules!

_____

_____

_____

_____

_____

_____

_____

_____

_____

_____

_____

_____

_____

_____

_____

_____

_____

_____

_____

KEY #1: RESILIENCE. How have you practiced resilience in the last month? What challenges have you faced, and how did you manage them?

WRITE ON! Make a list of three to five challenges or obstacles you've had to face in the last four weeks. How did you work through them? Write, read, reflect. What are you noticing about your own resilience-building strategies?

_____

_____

_____

_____

_____

_____

_____

_____

_____

_____

_____

_____

_____

_____

_____

_____

_____

_____

_____

_____

DESPAIR TO HOPE. A team at UC Berkeley noted that maintaining the same bedtime, even on weekends, is a key factor in managing anxiety. According to their study, "The best bridge between despair and hope is a good night's sleep."

WRITE ON! Write out your bedtime routine. Can you adjust it so that you can go to bed at about the same time each night? What would you have to do to sustain a new sleep habit?

THE BETTER-FEELING THOUGHT. Some thoughts are neutral and objective. Others are loaded with emotion. *Anxiety mindfulness* is a process of learning how to discern which thoughts are associated with unpleasant or exhausting feelings, and how different thoughts could result in better feelings.

WRITE ON! What are the kinds of feelings you would like to experience? Next to each, write a thought or two that could possibly produce the better feeling. Read back and reflect.

_____

_____

_____

_____

_____

WEEKLY REVIEW. Read over the week's entries, reflections, or both. How do you rank your anxiety this week? How do you rank your use of writing? How is the realistic progress of your intentions going? Are you noticing changes?

On a scale of 1 (low) to 7 (high), rate your week:

Anxiety?	①	②	③	④	⑤	⑥	⑦
Writing process?	①	②	③	④	⑤	⑥	⑦
Intentions?	①	②	③	④	⑤	⑥	⑦
Noticing shifts?	①	②	③	④	⑤	⑥	⑦

WRITE ON! Write observations as you rate your week. Note any connections you may see.

_____

_____

_____

_____

SETTING INTENTION. How are your intentions coming along? Is it getting easier to discern which are internally sourced and which are deadline driven or otherwise externally sourced? Both are fine to set as weekly intentions.

WRITE ON! What are three intentions for this week? Break larger intentions into week-size bites. Review last week's intentions. How are you doing?

_____

_____

_____

_____

_____

_____

YOUR INNER ALLY. We all have a mentor, a cheerleader, an advocate as a part of ourselves. Close your eyes and imagine who your inner ally might be. Is she/he someone you already know and trust? A heroic figure? Fictional character? Imaginary friend?

WRITE ON! Describe your inner ally in detail. What is your inner ally's personality? What does he/she want for you? How can your inner ally help?

_____

_____

_____

_____

_____

_____

_____

CUMULATIVE STRESS. Cognitive psychologist Dr. Edmund Bourne's research across 20 years leads to a conclusion that "anxiety disorders are an outcome of cumulative stress over time." The rise of technology and drastic shifts in economy and culture are significant contributors, he says.

WRITE ON! Divide a page into decades of your life. Within each decade, write down the personal and impersonal (e.g., technological) stressors. What do you notice about your cumulative stress?

KEY #2: OUTLOOK. Dr. Davidson's quality of outlook, you'll remember from Week 2, is whether you can see the good in the not-so-great. It's the practice of extending kindness to yourself and others when things are hard.

WRITE ON! Write a list of three to five times in the last few weeks that you've been gentle with yourself or compassionate with others. Choose at least one story and expand on it with sensory details. Read and reflect.

_____

_____

_____

_____

_____

_____

_____

_____

_____

_____

_____

_____

_____

_____

_____

_____

_____

_____

_____

POSSIBILITY THINKING. Emily Dickinson wrote, "I dwell in possibility. . . ." Susan Hansted of the Institute of Possibility Thinking says, "Possibility thinking works to break cycles of perception that drive behavior and evoke stressful emotional responses." With possibility thinking, "limiting beliefs fade away . . . [we] start to look at the world and our relationship to it differently."

WRITE ON! Dwell on possibility. What might be possible for you? Try a list, or a list poem.

_____

_____

_____

_____

_____

_____

_____

_____

_____

_____

_____

_____

_____

_____

_____

_____

_____

_____

_____

_____

_____

_____

IT'S NOT YOUR FAULT. Much of cumulative stress is beyond your control. We live in toxic times: a pandemic, political divisiveness, road rage, economic uncertainty, global terrorism, overwhelming demands on time, attention, and focus. This stress is inevitable, but it's not your fault.

WRITE ON! Start by writing, *"It's not my fault."* Follow your pen or keystrokes for 10 minutes. Write quickly. Read back and write a reflection.

_____

_____

_____

_____

_____

_____

_____

WEEKLY REVIEW. Read over the week's entries, reflections, or both. How do you rank your anxiety this week? How do you rank your use of writing? How is the realistic progress of your intentions going? Are you noticing changes?

On a scale of 1 (low) to 7 (high), rate your week:

Anxiety	①	②	③	④	⑤	⑥	⑦
Writing process?	①	②	③	④	⑤	⑥	⑦
Intentions?	①	②	③	④	⑤	⑥	⑦
Noticing shifts?	①	②	③	④	⑤	⑥	⑦

WRITE ON! Write observations as you rate your week. Note any connections you may see.

_____

_____

_____

_____

SETTING INTENTION. Let's set your intention for this week!

WRITE ON! What are three intentions for this week? These can be related to any area of your life. Review and reflect on last week's intentions.

_____

_____

_____

_____

_____

_____

_____

_____

_____

INNER ALLY AS PROBLEM SOLVER. Metaphors help us solve problems by letting us borrow the qualities embedded in the metaphor. Let's revisit your inner ally (Week 6) and let them help with problem solving!

WRITE ON! Bring to mind a current stress or anxiety. Write down the specific problem it represents. Invite your inner ally to write a letter to you with advice or suggestions. Or have a little conversation in which you write both parts. Read and reflect.

_____

_____

_____

_____

_____

_____

_____

_____

CAN YOU CHANGE THIS? An excellent question to ask yourself when you're feeling stuck or agitated is "Can I change this?" If there is a part of the situation that you can positively change, take action. If it's outside of your control, accept that all of your worry or over-focus won't make a difference.

WRITE ON! Go back to your "It's not my fault" write from last week. Note whether or not you can personally change anything you wrote about. If you can, make a plan. If you can't, write a release letter absolving yourself of responsibility.

_____

_____

_____

_____

_____

_____

_____

_____

_____

_____

_____

_____

_____

_____

_____

_____

_____

_____

_____

_____

KEY #3: ATTENTION. How is the quality of your attention these last weeks? Pioneering journal therapist and depth psychologist Dr. Ira Progoff said one of the functions of the journal is to "savor the beauty and stare straight into the pain." What beauty have you savored? What pain have you stared into?

WRITE ON! Write a list of three to five times lately you've paid attention to beauty or pain. Write those stories. Include sensory details.

_____

_____

_____

_____

_____

_____

_____

_____

_____

_____

_____

_____

_____

_____

_____

_____

_____

_____

_____

_____

_____

COGNITIVE THERAPY. Psychiatrist Aaron Beck, founder of cognitive-behavioral therapy, says its basic assumption is that you can "reduce negative feelings like anxiety by changing emotion-related thoughts, beliefs, and attitudes."

WRITE ON! Write a list of about 10 thoughts, beliefs, and attitudes that contribute to anxiety, tension, worry, or fear. Leave space between each. What might a better-feeling thought be? Write it underneath, along with the better feeling.

PRACTICE: 5-4-3-2-1. The best time to practice grounding techniques is when you already feel grounded. But if you're feeling unsettled, then this will likely help! Center yourself with deep breathing.

WRITE ON! In sensory detail, write five things you see, four things you can touch, three things you hear, two things you smell, and one thing you taste. Read back, savor, and reflect. How do you feel?

_____

_____

_____

_____

_____

_____

_____

WEEKLY REVIEW. Read over the week's entries, reflections, or both. How do you rank your anxiety this week? How do you rank your use of writing? How is the progress of your intentions going? Are you noticing changes?

On a scale of 1 (low) to 7 (high), rate your week:

Anxiety?	①	②	③	④	⑤	⑥	⑦
Writing process?	①	②	③	④	⑤	⑥	⑦
Intentions?	①	②	③	④	⑤	⑥	⑦
Noticing shifts?	①	②	③	④	⑤	⑥	⑦

WRITE ON! Write observations as you rate your week. Note any connections you may see.

_____

_____

_____

_____

SETTING INTENTION. Eight weeks in, your weekly intention-setting is becoming a habit. Starting now, every time you continue writing weekly intentions, the practice will deepen and become more natural. Don't forget to review your prior week's intentions to harvest success!

WRITE ON! What are three intentions for this week? Keep them specific enough that you can make observable progress in a week.

_____

_____

_____

_____

_____

_____

_____

YOUR SUPERPOWER. We might not be able to cast Spider-Man webs from our palms, but everybody's got superpowers. Often they hide in plain sight. Maybe you're a good listener, or you're great at organizing, or you create lovely spaces.

WRITE ON! Make a list of things you're naturally good at. Choose one and write about it. How might it help you manage stressful situations? Read and reflect.

_____

_____

_____

_____

_____

_____

_____

_____

WHAT DIDN'T HAPPEN? Here's an Eight-Word Tip from Boyd: Most of what you worry about never happens.

WRITE ON! Think of a time you worried about something that never happened. Write that story. Read back and reflect. What are your takeaways?

_____

_____

_____

_____

_____

_____

_____

_____

_____

_____

_____

_____

_____

_____

_____

_____

_____

_____

_____

_____

_____

_____

_____

KEY #4: GENEROSITY. Think back over the last week or two. How have you been generous?

WRITE ON! Make a list of three to five experiences of your own generosity. Remember that generosity can be gifts of heart, service, prayers, or good thoughts for others. Choose one and write its story. Read and reflect.

_____

_____

_____

_____

_____

_____

_____

_____

_____

_____

_____

_____

_____

_____

_____

_____

_____

_____

_____

_____

_____

_____

_____

_____

COGNITIVE DISTORTIONS. Cognitive distortions are thoughts that reflexively appear under stress. All-or-nothing thinking, catastrophizing, jumping to conclusions—these are all thought patterns that think us. Good news: You can unlearn these cognitive habits and replace them with better-feeling thoughts.

WRITE ON! What are some unwanted thought patterns that persist in you—that you seem to not have control over? Read back and reflect on whether there is actual evidence to support the truth of these thoughts.

WORRY WINDOW. Set aside a 15-minute segment of your day specifically as a worry window. During that time, you can worry about anything you want. Until your appointed worry window, accumulate worries on a list.

WRITE ON! Review the list during your allotted time. How many of these worries, as Boyd (Day 3) suggested, worked themselves out?

_____

_____

_____

_____

_____

_____

WEEKLY REVIEW. Read over the week's entries, reflections, or both. How do you rank your anxiety this week? How do you rank your use of writing? How is the progress of your intentions going? Are you noticing changes?

On a scale of 1 (low) to 7 (high), rate your week:

Anxiety?	①	②	③	④	⑤	⑥	⑦
Writing process?	①	②	③	④	⑤	⑥	⑦
Intentions?	①	②	③	④	⑤	⑥	⑦
Noticing shifts?	①	②	③	④	⑤	⑥	⑦

WRITE ON! Write observations as you rate your week. Note any connections you may see.

_____

_____

_____

_____

_____

SETTING INTENTION. It's time to set weekly intentions and review last week's!

WRITE ON! What are three intentions for this week? These can be related to any area of your life. Break larger intentions into week-size bites.

_____

_____

_____

_____

_____

_____

_____

_____

PRACTICE: SUPERPOWER. Last week you wrote about your superpowers—the things you naturally do well. Part of anxiety mindfulness is recognizing, in real time, when you are operating from a place of strength and competence.

WRITE ON! Choose one of your superpowers and write about how it has shown up in the last several days. Were you aware of it at the time? Did your awareness shift anything?

_____

_____

_____

_____

_____

_____

_____

_____

WORRY WINDOW IN ACTION. Michele reports that when worry starts to interfere with her sleep or daily tasks, she schedules a worry window. "Usually most of my list is resolved. It shows me the inflated nature of anxiety," she reports.

WRITE ON! Make a list (or a list poem) of your specific worry categories—the ones that repeat themselves over and over. Name them like *Friends* episodes: "The One About Leaving the Burner On." "The One About Looking Foolish."

KEY #1: RESILIENCE. Each of us brings innate resources—much like superpowers—to help us develop resilience. You might be a naturally patient person. You might have a sense of humor that helps you cope. You might be stubborn. Thinking back over your life, what are your superpowers of resilience?

WRITE ON! Explore the skills you bring to resilience. How have these skills and traits served you? How can they serve you now?

_____

_____

_____

_____

_____

_____

_____

_____

_____

_____

_____

_____

_____

_____

_____

_____

_____

_____

_____

_____

_____

_____

_____

_____

ALL-OR-NOTHING THINKING. Last week we wrote about cognitive distortions. We'll now explore some of them, one by one. All-or-nothing thinking warps reality. It makes the assumption that anything that isn't a total success must be a total failure. Any critique or redirection is used as evidence of a flop.

WRITE ON! Write down examples of all-or-nothing thinking from your own life. Then step back and evaluate. Which are realistically true? Which are exaggerations?

_____

_____

_____

_____

_____

_____

_____

_____

_____

_____

_____

_____

_____

_____

_____

_____

_____

_____

_____

_____

_____

_____

_____

DATE _____   **WEEK 9 • DAY 6**

TOUCHBACK: HYDRATION. How's your water consumption? Can you add a glass per day?
One way to stay both hydrated and relaxed is to take long showers or baths. While you're
immersing, practice some creative visualization: Your stress is washing down the drain,
or you're cleansed of anxious thoughts.

WRITE ON! Write your own metaphors for the bath or shower. Then practice them!

_____

_____

_____

_____

_____

_____

DATE _____   **WEEK 9 • DAY 7**

WEEKLY REVIEW. Read over the week's entries, reflections, or both. How do you rank your
anxiety this week? How do you rank your use of writing? How is the progress of your
intentions going? Are you noticing changes?

On a scale of 1 (low) to 7 (high), rate your week:

Anxiety?	① ② ③ ④ ⑤ ⑥ ⑦
Writing process?	① ② ③ ④ ⑤ ⑥ ⑦
Intentions?	① ② ③ ④ ⑤ ⑥ ⑦
Noticing shifts?	① ② ③ ④ ⑤ ⑥ ⑦

WRITE ON! Write observations as you rate your week. Note any connections you may see.

_____

_____

_____

_____

_____

SETTING INTENTION. It's Intentions Day!

WRITE ON! What are three intentions for this week? See if you can include at least one you're genuinely excited about.

_____

_____

_____

_____

_____

_____

_____

_____

_____

SAFE PLACE. Your self-regulation toolkit includes reliable ways to quickly retreat from anxious thoughts and behaviors. An internal "safe place" gives instant transport to a place where you can shift from ramping up to chilling out.

WRITE ON! Bring to mind or imagine a place that feels calm, safe, and peaceful. Is it in nature? Your home? A place you've been? A place you make up? Sit, breathe, explore the image. Then write in sensory detail.

_____

_____

_____

_____

_____

_____

_____

BOX BREATHING. The Mayo Clinic recommends intentional deep breathing to calm and regulate anxiety. One simple breathwork technique is "box breathing." Inhale deeply to a count of four. Hold to a four count. Exhale to a four count. Hold again to a four count. Repeat three times.

WRITE ON! Start by writing three feeling words or phrases (emotional or/and physical). Practice four sets of box breathing. Then write three more feeling words or phrases. What do you notice?

_____

_____

_____

_____

_____

_____

_____

_____

_____

_____

_____

_____

_____

_____

_____

_____

_____

_____

KEY #2: OUTLOOK. An aspect of outlook in Dr. Davidson's research is our capacity to assume positive intent in others. Some indigenous cultures call this the praiseworthy core of a person or situation. If there is even a kernel of goodness somewhere, find it and praise it.

WRITE ON! Bring to mind a difficult experience. What is its praiseworthy core?

PROACTIVE PANIC. Stacie proactively manages a panic attack: "I use my Fitbit to monitor my heart rate. It gives me a head start if I begin to have a panic attack. I can remove myself from my environment, or pull off the road if I'm driving, to practice breathing or other self-care."

WRITE ON! What are your earliest signs of panic or anxiety? What is the self-care you'll practice to get in front of it?

_____

_____

_____

_____

_____

_____

_____

_____

_____

_____

_____

_____

_____

_____

_____

_____

_____

_____

_____

_____

_____

ALL YOU NEED IS BREATH. From Healthline Media comes this nifty acronym:

B = Box breathing (see Day 3)

R = Roll your shoulders; stretch

E = Extend your clasped hands overhead

A = Adjust your posture (tall and straight)

T = Talk about it, *or,* Tell your journal

H = Hydrate—drink water

WRITE ON! Try this sequence. Tell your journal what you notice!

_____

_____

_____

_____

_____

WEEKLY REVIEW. Read over the week's entries, reflections, or both. How do you rank your anxiety this week? How do you rank your use of writing? How is the progress of your intentions going? Are you noticing changes?

On a scale of 1 (low) to 7 (high), rate your week:

Anxiety?   ① ② ③ ④ ⑤ ⑥ ⑦

Writing process?   ① ② ③ ④ ⑤ ⑥ ⑦

Intentions?   ① ② ③ ④ ⑤ ⑥ ⑦

Noticing shifts?   ① ② ③ ④ ⑤ ⑥ ⑦

WRITE ON! Write observations as you rate your week. Note any connections you may see.

_____

_____

_____

SETTING INTENTION. Intentions are goals that are internally sourced. We want them not only for what they represent (a met deadline, a completed project, a shift in thinking or feeling) but also for how we'll feel (content, satisfied, regulated) as we move toward them.

WRITE ON! What are three intentions for this week? Did you achieve your "excitement" intention from last week?

_____

_____

_____

_____

_____

_____

_____

_____

LIVING THROUGH METAPHOR. Keep your inner ally, your superpowers, and your safe place with you as you approach daily problems. Suddenly paralyzed with worry or shaking with fear? Visualize yourself and your inner ally in your safe place, strategizing ways to invoke your superpowers in this situation.

WRITE ON! Make up some scenarios wherein you and your inner ally are in your safe place. Which superpower would be called upon for each scene? How would it play out?

_____

_____

_____

_____

_____

CLASSICAL MUSIC. A Turkish research team studied the effects of classical music on anxiety and well-being. Subjects who listened to classical music for 60 consecutive days showed a statistically significant decrease in "trait" (enduring) anxiety.

WRITE ON! The Proprioceptive Writing method uses baroque music (60 beats per minute) to induce a receptive state. Put on classical music, ideally with about 60 beats per minute, and write for 10 to 15 minutes. Choose your own prompt. Read and reflect on what you notice.

KEY #3: ATTENTION. Part of attention is focus. Dr. Davidson quotes 19th-century psychologist William James: "The ability to bring back a wandering mind again and again is the very root of judgment, character, and will." Let's practice the well-being key of focus.

WRITE ON! Make a bullet list of things on your mind. Choose one. Switch your phone to DO NOT DISTURB and set the timer for seven minutes. Then write, gently disregarding anything that pulls your focus away from writing. Read and reflect. What did you notice?

_____
_____
_____
_____
_____
_____
_____
_____
_____
_____
_____
_____
_____
_____
_____
_____
_____
_____
_____
_____

OVERGENERALIZATION. This cognitive distortion is the perception that any mistake or defeat is part of a constant, never-ending pattern. Stay alert to self-talk that includes the signal words *always* and *never*.

WRITE ON! Finish the sentence stems, "I always . . ." and "I never . . ." three or four times each. Take any two that you recognize as habituated thoughts and challenge them. What are the "sometimes" exceptions to your "always/never's"?

_____

_____

_____

_____

_____

_____

_____

_____

_____

_____

_____

_____

_____

_____

_____

_____

_____

_____

_____

_____

RELATIONSHIP WITH BREATH. Like water, your body depends on breath for its survival. Although anyone can stay alive with shallow chest breathing, a deepened breath is an invitation to a deepened relationship with self.

WRITE ON! Write a love letter—or, if you prefer, a love poem—to your breath.

_____

_____

_____

_____

_____

_____

_____

_____

WEEKLY REVIEW. Read over the week's entries, reflections, or both. How do you rank your anxiety this week? How do you rank your use of writing? How is the progress of your intentions going? Are you noticing changes?

On a scale of 1 (low) to 7 (high), rate your week:

Anxiety?	①	②	③	④	⑤	⑥	⑦
Writing process?	①	②	③	④	⑤	⑥	⑦
Intentions?	①	②	③	④	⑤	⑥	⑦
Noticing shifts?	①	②	③	④	⑤	⑥	⑦

WRITE ON! Write observations as you rate your week. Note any connections you may see.

_____

_____

_____

_____

SETTING INTENTION. Are there carry-over intentions from prior weeks that you'd like to revisit?

WRITE ON! Write three intentions this week, including any that you'd like to carry forward.

_____

_____

_____

_____

_____

_____

_____

THE PROPRIOCEPTIVE QUESTION. In addition to writing to baroque music (60 beats per minute), the Proprioceptive Writing method asks the "proprioceptive question, " which is, "What do I mean by that?"

WRITE ON! Write about something that is on your mind. When you notice yourself falling into a familiar unproductive thought pattern, drop down a line, center yourself, and ask, "What do I mean by that?" Pause, drop down another line, and respond honestly. Continue and repeat the question as needed.

_____

_____

_____

_____

_____

_____

_____

VIBRATIONS OF SOUND. For Baiba, singing or working with her voice is a touchstone for anxiety management. "Vocalizing allows my body to feel the vibrations of the sounds it creates," she says.

WRITE ON! Find a place where you won't be interrupted. Experiment with your voice by singing or vocalizing. Locate the vibrations in your body. Write about what you notice.

KEY #4: GENEROSITY. Your generosity may be expressed in acts of service. When you volunteer time, money, energy, talent, or skill to your community, it is an act of generosity.

WRITE ON! List the causes you serve and how you serve them. How does it feel to be generous? How does this feeling contribute to your self-esteem and sense of well-being?

_____

_____

_____

_____

_____

_____

_____

_____

_____

_____

_____

_____

_____

_____

_____

_____

_____

_____

_____

_____

_____

_____

PRACTICE: BOX BREATHING AND BREATH. As we have discussed, both anxiety treatment and mindfulness emphasize the importance of deep breathing. It is one of the most reliable ways to regain emotional control and be receptive to better-feeling thoughts.

WRITE ON! Practice Week 10's box breathing and BREATH techniques. Write and reflect. What do you notice?

YOUR SOUNDTRACK. Did you try vocalizing (Day 3)? Your own special music can resonate with a similar vibrational effect on you as that of singing or chanting.

WRITE ON! What's your soundtrack? What songs, artists, or compositions put you in deep alignment? Listen to a cut from your soundtrack and write about its story in your life.

_____

_____

_____

_____

_____

_____

_____

_____

WEEKLY REVIEW. Read over the week's entries, reflections, or both. How do you rank your anxiety this week? How do you rank your use of writing? How is the progress of your intentions going? Are you noticing changes?

On a scale of 1 (low) to 7 (high), rate your week:

Anxiety?	①	②	③	④	⑤	⑥	⑦
Writing process?	①	②	③	④	⑤	⑥	⑦
Intentions?	①	②	③	④	⑤	⑥	⑦
Noticing shifts?	①	②	③	④	⑤	⑥	⑦

WRITE ON! Write observations as you rate your week. Note any connections you may see.

_____

_____

_____

_____

INTENTIONS IN REVIEW. In this quarter, you've set intentions for your week. You've been working on breaking big goals or intentions into week-size bites.

WRITE ON! Write about what you've learned from setting intentions each week. Are you evolving as you go, letting yourself learn how to adjust based on experience? Are you discovering what a reasonable weekly goal looks like? Write and reflect.

_____

_____

_____

_____

_____

_____

_____

WRITING IN REVIEW. How have the writing processes and reflection writes contributed to your learning about yourself, anxiety, and mindfulness?

WRITE ON! Which writing techniques and practices have been especially useful? What did you learn or deepen? How about the reflection writes? Write, read back, and reflect.

_____

_____

_____

_____

_____

_____

_____

_____

SCIENCE IN REVIEW. Which scientific explorations (such as Davidson's four keys or the cognitive-behavioral thinking distortions) most captured your attention or imagination?

WRITE ON! Reflect on what you learned or reinforced from the research and science explorations this quarter.

_____

_____

_____

_____

_____

_____

_____

_____

_____

_____

_____

_____

_____

_____

_____

_____

_____

_____

_____

_____

_____

_____

_____

KEYS: THE FOUR KEYS IN REVIEW. How have the four keys of well-being (resilience, outlook, attention, generosity) shown up in your life this quarter?

WRITE ON! What is shifting for you in any of these areas? Are you noticing changes in your thinking or process? Write and reflect.

_____

_____

_____

_____

_____

_____

_____

_____

_____

_____

_____

_____

_____

_____

_____

_____

_____

_____

_____

_____

MINDFULNESS IN REVIEW. What do you notice in the area of mindfulness this quarter? What strategies have you learned?

WRITE ON! Reflect on your awareness, attention, and practice of mindfulness techniques learned or reinforced this quarter.

WEEKLY REVIEWS. How well have the weekly reviews helped you observe and track your anxiety, writing, intentions, and outcomes?

WRITE ON! Write about any observations or correlations you have made from Week 1 until now. Reflect on any insights or surprises.

_____

_____

_____

_____

_____

QUARTERLY REVIEW. How do you rank your anxiety for the last 13 weeks? How do you rank your use of writing? How about your intentions? Are you noticing changes?

On a scale of 1 (low) to 7 (high), rate the entire first quarter:

Anxiety?	① ② ③ ④ ⑤ ⑥ ⑦
Writing process?	① ② ③ ④ ⑤ ⑥ ⑦
Intentions?	① ② ③ ④ ⑤ ⑥ ⑦
Noticing shifts?	① ② ③ ④ ⑤ ⑥ ⑦

WRITE ON! Synthesize the past 13 weeks. What have been your major takeaways? Where do you feel as if you're struggling or vulnerable? What have you not yet been able to put into practice? Assess your progress, remembering to be gentle with yourself.

_____

_____

_____

_____

_____

SETTING INTENTION. The weekly process of setting intentions brings focus and action orientation to your days. Be sure that your intentions are framed in positive language. Specify what you want rather than what you want to avoid.

WRITE ON! What are three intentions for this week? These can be related to any area of your life.

_____

_____

_____

_____

_____

_____

_____

_____

_____

_____

_____

_____

_____

_____

_____

_____

_____

_____

_____

_____

_____

_____

STRUCTURED WRITE. When structure meets sentence stem, the result is the structured write. This series of seven sentence stems develop into a cohesive story. Write a sentence or two for each stem.

WRITE ON! The basic seven-part form takes 10 to 15 minutes. Practice on an "every-day normal" problem, a chronic annoyance that typically isn't anxiety inducing.

"I want to write about . . ." _____

_____

_____

"The first thing that comes to mind . . ." _____

_____

_____

"Below the surface, I find . . ." _____

_____

_____

"The challenge here is . . ." _____

_____

_____

"In order to move forward, I . . ." _____

_____

_____

"I can ask for help/support from . . ." _____

_____

_____

"My next step is . . ." _____

_____

_____

DATE _____   WEEK **14** • DAY **3**

FIGHT OR FLIGHT. According to the American Institute of Stress, the fight-or-flight response is a near-instantaneous physiological reaction to something perceived as physically *or mentally* dangerous. Calming your system can take 20 to 60 minutes.

WRITE ON! We can't stop our bodies from responding to perceived dangers, but we can train our minds to recover. Write your way to balance. Assure yourself that you've had a scare but you're safe, aware, breathing.

_____

_____

_____

_____

_____

_____

_____

DATE _____   WEEK **14** • DAY **4**

KEY #1: RESILIENCE. How have you practiced resilience in the last several weeks? What challenges and stresses have you leaned into? How did you manage them?

WRITE ON! Make a list of three to five challenges, stresses, or obstacles you've faced over the last few weeks. What did you do (or not do) that helped you cope? What are you learning about yourself and resilience?

_____

_____

_____

_____

_____

_____

_____

CALM-DOWN QUOTES. Deana says that journal writing calms her if she's having a panic attack. "I can just write nonsense until I start to calm down," she says. When she shifts into better control, Deana flips to a list of "calm-down quotes" she keeps in the front of her journal.

WRITE ON! Start a list of calm-down quotations (e.g., "This too shall pass," reassuring things your mother used to say, lines of poetry or verses from sacred texts) in the front of your journal. Update often.

_____

_____

_____

_____

_____

_____

_____

_____

_____

_____

_____

_____

_____

_____

_____

_____

_____

_____

WHY WRITING WORKS. You've been writing for about three months now. Perhaps you've noticed that writing is helping. Over the next few months, we'll explore why it is that writing works as a cognitive, behavioral, emotional, and mindfulness tool.

WRITE ON! What are you noticing so far about the effectiveness of your writing?

_____

_____

_____

_____

_____

_____

_____

WEEKLY REVIEW. Read over the week's entries, reflections, or both. How do you rank your anxiety this week? How do you rank your use of these writing processes? How is the progress of your intentions going? Are you noticing changes?

On a scale of 1 (low) to 7 (high), rate your week:

Anxiety?	① ② ③ ④ ⑤ ⑥ ⑦
Writing process?	① ② ③ ④ ⑤ ⑥ ⑦
Intentions?	① ② ③ ④ ⑤ ⑥ ⑦
Noticing shifts?	① ② ③ ④ ⑤ ⑥ ⑦

WRITE ON! Write observations as you rate your week. Note any connections you may see.

_____

_____

_____

_____

_____

SETTING INTENTION. Be sure to frame your intentions in positive language. Specify what you want rather than what you want to avoid.

WRITE ON! What are three intentions for this week?

_____

_____

_____

_____

_____

_____

_____

_____

_____

CLUSTERING (MIND MAPPING). Clustering is an association of thoughts and feelings from a central word or phrase. Write a word in the middle of a page and circle it. Then, spin thoughts off of other thoughts to write associated words surrounding it, connecting with circles and lines, returning to the center for fresh associations.

WRITE ON! Use *anxiety* or *mindfulness*, or a topic on your mind. Work quickly. Don't edit or censor, just get it down. Shift into visual review. Write a synthesis of what you see.

_____

_____

_____

_____

_____

_____

_____

_____

SLEEPING DEEPLY. Deep sleep is now validated as "most apt to calm and reset an anxious brain," says Dr. Matthew Walker, co-author of a 2019 sleep study. To get more deep sleep, power down bright lights and avoid screen time for at least an hour before bed.

WRITE ON! Make a list of relaxing activities (e.g., music, herbal tea, stretching, journaling, a bath) you could use to power down your day for more deep sleep. Which will you try tonight?

_____

_____

_____

_____

_____

_____

_____

_____

_____

_____

_____

_____

_____

_____

_____

_____

_____

_____

_____

KEY #2: OUTLOOK. Are you more able to see the silver linings in the clouds of your past few weeks? Are you being gentle with yourself and others?

WRITE ON! Write a list of times in the past few weeks you've been gentle with yourself or others. Choose at least one story and write it out with sensory detail.

_____

_____

_____

_____

_____

_____

_____

_____

_____

_____

_____

_____

_____

_____

_____

_____

_____

_____

_____

_____

MEDITATION AUDIOS. Dimitri sends himself off to sleep each night with meditation audios designed for tranquil sleep. "I immediately go into a hypnotic state of relaxation, then fall asleep before the audio is complete." He notes, "I feel significantly more rested on mornings after I use the audios, and I'm clearer and calmer."

WRITE ON! What consistently gives you the best night of sleep? What consistently keeps you awake?

_____

_____

_____

_____

_____

_____

_____

_____

_____

_____

_____

_____

_____

_____

_____

_____

_____

_____

_____

_____

_____

_____

_____

_____

WHY WRITING WORKS: IMMEDIACY. Your journal is available at 3:00 A.M., in the doctor's waiting room, in the middle of a panic attack. Its immediacy offers you much-needed control in calm-down situations.

WRITE ON! What circumstances are predictably difficult for you? How might your journal's immediacy and availability support you in these times?

_____

_____

_____

_____

_____

_____

WEEKLY REVIEW. Read over the week's entries, reflections, or both. How do you rank your anxiety this week? How do you rank your use of these writing processes? How is the progress of your intentions going? Are you noticing changes?

On a scale of 1 (low) to 7 (high), rate your week:

Anxiety?	1	2	3	4	5	6	7
Writing process?	1	2	3	4	5	6	7
Intentions?	1	2	3	4	5	6	7
Noticing shifts?	1	2	3	4	5	6	7

WRITE ON! Write observations as you rate your week. Note any connections you may see.

_____

_____

_____

_____

_____

SETTING INTENTION. Are there carry-over intentions from prior weeks that you'd like to revisit?

WRITE ON! Write three intentions this week, including any that you'd like to carry forward.

_____

_____

_____

_____

_____

_____

_____

_____

QUICK AND EASY. You've now learned six different writing techniques: the five-minute sprint, sentence stems, list poems, the structured write, clustering, and the reflection write. In this group, writes are typically short (5 to 15 minutes). The techniques themselves are quick and easy—short, structured, paced, contained, accessible, and straightforward.

WRITE ON! Which of these techniques are becoming parts of your regular toolkit? Anything you don't care for? Review your outcomes.

_____

_____

_____

_____

_____

_____

_____

GO-TO COMFORTS. We all have our go-to comforts—a long conversation with a best friend, Ben & Jerry's Cherry Garcia, chamomile tea, binge-watching Netflix—you've got your own.

WRITE ON! What are your go-to comforts? What reliably helps you feel safe, structured, secure? Make a list. Choose one that consistently works, and write for five to seven minutes about its role in your self-soothing.

_____

_____

_____

_____

_____

_____

_____

_____

_____

_____

_____

_____

_____

_____

_____

_____

_____

_____

_____

_____

_____

KEY #3: ATTENTION. To what are you paying attention in recent weeks?

WRITE ON! Check in with yourself on your attention.

SOOTHE THE SOUL WITH POETRY. Poetry therapy, a recognized creative arts therapy, uses literature and imagination for emotional wellness. Poets frequently used by poetry therapists include Mary Oliver, William Stafford, Naomi Shihab Nye, and Billy Collins.

WRITE ON! If you're not familiar with any of these poets, an Internet search will give you many leads. When you find a poem that resonates, choose any line or image that moves you and use it as a springboard for writing.

_____

_____

_____

_____

_____

_____

_____

_____

_____

_____

_____

_____

_____

_____

_____

_____

_____

_____

_____

_____

WHY WRITING WORKS: EMOTIONAL MANAGEMENT. The important work of anxiety mindfulness brings with it a host of perfectly normal, if difficult, feelings. Your journal absorbs these feelings without judgment, censure, or reprisal. As a bonus, your catharsis often brings clarity and insight.

WRITE ON! What one feeling is the most difficult for you? How do you manage that feeling?

_____

_____

_____

_____

_____

_____

WEEKLY REVIEW. Read over the week's entries, reflections, or both. How do you rank your anxiety this week? How do you rank your use of these writing processes? How is the progress of your intentions going? Are you noticing changes?

On a scale of 1 (low) to 7 (high), rate your week:

Anxiety?	①	②	③	④	⑤	⑥	⑦
Writing process?	①	②	③	④	⑤	⑥	⑦
Intentions?	①	②	③	④	⑤	⑥	⑦
Noticing shifts?	①	②	③	④	⑤	⑥	⑦

WRITE ON! Write observations as you rate your week. Note any connections you may see.

_____

_____

_____

_____

SETTING INTENTION. The weekly process of setting intentions brings focus and action orientation to your days. Be sure that your intentions are framed in positive language. Specify what you want rather than what you want to avoid.

WRITE ON! What are three intentions for this week? These can be related to any area of your life. Break larger intentions into week-size bites.

_____

_____

_____

_____

_____

_____

_____

THE METAPHOR GAME. Start with a list of about 10 metaphors: animal, food, weather condition, color, shape, shoes, landscape, building, texture, furniture, or substitute your own.

WRITE ON! Complete the sentence stems with *anxiety*: "If anxiety were building, it would be a rat-infested crack house." Continue with the same metaphors in the same order, using *mindfulness*. Read both lists, compare, and reflect.

_____

_____

_____

_____

_____

_____

_____

MINDFULNESS METAPHORS. From yesterday's mindfulness metaphors, draw out one or two that give you the most vivid imagery or positive visceral response. Practice the Relaxation Response (Week 2) or box breathing (Week 10) as you visualize mindfulness as your chosen metaphor(s). Note how your body feels.

WRITE ON! Write your responses to the visualization. How does this mindfulness metaphor feel in your body? What is your physical response?

_____

_____

_____

_____

_____

_____

_____

_____

_____

_____

_____

_____

_____

_____

_____

_____

_____

_____

_____

_____

KEY #4: GENEROSITY. Think back over the last few weeks. How have you been generous?

WRITE ON! Make a list of three to five experiences of your own generosity. Choose one and write its story.

_____

_____

_____

_____

_____

_____

_____

_____

_____

_____

_____

_____

_____

_____

_____

_____

_____

_____

_____

_____

_____

_____

_____

_____

ADVENTURES WITH ANXIETY. Video game developer Nicky Case created a choose-your-own-adventure game that casts anxiety as a pet wolf. The user is guided through what Case describes as "basically one big augmented self-reflection tool" to identify, express, and reflect on deepest fears and the new relationship with these fears that the game helps develop.

WRITE ON! Return to Week 17, Day 2's anxiety metaphors. Which one(s) could you use as a way to create a new relationship with anxiety?

WHY WRITING WORKS: ACCEPTANCE. As one journal writer said, "My journal is the arche-typal friend. It's always waiting for me, totally accepting, and present. I can ignore it and discount its value and it never takes offense. I never have to start over or apologize. What a gift!"

WRITE ON! Write about how it feels, or might feel, to be completely accepted, just exactly as you are.

_____

_____

_____

_____

_____

_____

WEEKLY REVIEW. Read over the week's entries, reflections, or both. How do you rank your anxiety this week? How do you rank your use of these writing processes? How is the progress of your intentions going? Are you noticing changes?

On a scale of 1 (low) to 7 (high), rate your week:

Anxiety?	①	②	③	④	⑤	⑥	⑦
Writing process?	①	②	③	④	⑤	⑥	⑦
Intentions?	①	②	③	④	⑤	⑥	⑦
Noticing shifts?	①	②	③	④	⑤	⑥	⑦

WRITE ON! Write observations as you rate your week. Note any connections you may see.

_____

_____

_____

_____

_____

SETTING INTENTION. Keeping your weekly intentions in positive language helps with attention, the third key to well-being.

WRITE ON! What are three intentions for this week?

_____

_____

_____

_____

_____

_____

_____

_____

_____

_____

CAPTURED MOMENT. The journal technique of captured moment utilizes a short, sensory-based vignette to capture an intensely positive experience in words. Captured moments are great for "flash-freezing" peak experiences of peace, joy, insight, intimacy.

WRITE ON! Think about a time when you felt awake and alive, paired with a wash of positive emotion. It can be dramatic (summiting a mountain) or intimate (giving the baby a bath) or everyday (coffee on the porch at sunrise). Write for 7 to 10 minutes with lots of sensory detail.

_____

_____

_____

_____

_____

_____

HOW DOES YOUR GARDEN GROW? A Korean research study demonstrated that horticulture therapy decreased anxiety and fatigue and increased quality of life in patients with mood disorders. Gardening is a natural antidote to anxiety: It's grounding, sensory, and creative. The results are aesthetic (daisies!) or functional (tomatoes!). Gardening also teaches patience, hope, and possibilities. If you don't have a patch of land to dig in, try growing herbs in a kitchen window or pot a houseplant.

WRITE ON! Write a captured moment about a positive experience in a garden.

KEY #1: RESILIENCE. How have you managed challenges in the past several weeks? Check in with resilience skills and strategies. How are you falling down and getting back up? What are you learning?

WRITE ON! Explore the skills you bring to resilience. How have these skills and traits served you? How can they serve you now?

_____

_____

_____

_____

_____

_____

_____

_____

_____

_____

_____

_____

_____

_____

_____

_____

_____

_____

_____

_____

_____

_____

_____

_____

THE GUT-BRAIN AXIS. Dr. Uma Naidoo, a Harvard psychiatrist who is also a chef, notes that 95% of serotonin receptors are found in the lining of the gut. Thus, she says, healthy eating and probiotics may be natural remedies for anxiety and depression.

WRITE ON! What is your nutritional profile? To what extent do you prioritize healthy eating?

WHY WRITING WORKS: TRACKING CYCLES AND PATTERNS. Our habituated behaviors either promote wellness or contribute to discomfort. When you write, you create a behavioral database that can be used to track trends toward wellness or stress.

WRITE ON! In the writing you've done so far, have you started noticing cycles and patterns?

_____

_____

_____

_____

_____

_____

_____

WEEKLY REVIEW. Read over the week's entries, reflections, or both. How do you rank your anxiety this week? How do you rank your use of these writing processes? How is the progress of your intentions going? Are you noticing changes?

On a scale of 1 (low) to 7 (high), rate your week:

Anxiety?	①	②	③	④	⑤	⑥	⑦
Writing process?	①	②	③	④	⑤	⑥	⑦
Intentions?	①	②	③	④	⑤	⑥	⑦
Noticing shifts?	①	②	③	④	⑤	⑥	⑦

WRITE ON! Write observations as you rate your week. Note any connections you may see.

_____

_____

_____

_____

SETTING INTENTION. Let's set intentions for the week!

WRITE ON! What are three intentions for this week? Perhaps by now you are in a rhythm of breaking a longer vision into week-size intentions and carrying the vision forward week by week.

_____

_____

_____

_____

_____

_____

_____

_____

MINDFULNESS PANTRY. Let's revisit your mindfulness pantry, where you store your resources. You last wrote about this in Week 2. What tools and resources have you deepened or added to your pantry in the last few months?

WRITE ON! Take inventory of your mindfulness pantry. What was there before that has expanded? What new supplies have been added? Is anything in need of restocking?

_____

_____

_____

_____

_____

_____

_____

PRACTICE, PRACTICE, PRACTICE. Lucille, a mindfulness meditation practitioner for most of her adult life, offers her Ten-Word Tip: "Meditation's called a practice because you must practice, practice, practice."

WRITE ON! As you're contemplating yesterday's mindfulness pantry, is there something on the shelf that could use some practice, practice, practice? How might you bring it to the foreground? Read back and reflect with attention to an action plan.

KEY #2: OUTLOOK. Dr. Davidson emphasizes that outlook includes savoring a positive experience, as you might savor an extraordinary meal—slowing down and taking in the goodness through all your sensory channels. Practice savoring this month.

WRITE ON! Think of a recent experience that filled you with calm, joy, connection, nurturing, or pleasure. Close your eyes and focus on savoring the moment. Now write a vivid description from your senses.

YOUR ANTI-ANXIETY DIET: MAGNESIUM. Harvard's nutritional psychiatrist Dr. Naidoo reports that diets low in magnesium increased anxiety-related behaviors in mice, leading to the hypothesis that foods naturally rich in magnesium might help one feel calmer. She suggests adding magnesium-rich spinach, Swiss chard, legumes, nuts, and seeds to your diet.

WRITE ON! Write about your comfort foods. What are they? When do you eat them? Do they soothe or calm you emotionally, physically, or both?

WHY WRITING WORKS: GETTING TO KNOW YOUR "PARTS." We're each made up of many "parts," sometimes called subpersonalities or inner aspects. Your journal can help you identify and articulate these parts (e.g., the inner ally, inner critic, inner wisdom) and put them to use for good in your world.

WRITE ON! What "parts" of yourself are you familiar with? How might writing help you enhance or deepen the relationship with these parts?

_____

_____

_____

_____

_____

_____

_____

WEEKLY REVIEW. Read over the week's entries, reflections, or both. How do you rank your anxiety this week? How do you rank your use of these writing processes? How is the progress of your intentions going? Are you noticing changes?

On a scale of 1 (low) to 7 (high), rate your week:

Anxiety	①	②	③	④	⑤	⑥	⑦
Writing process?	①	②	③	④	⑤	⑥	⑦
Intentions?	①	②	③	④	⑤	⑥	⑦
Noticing shifts?	①	②	③	④	⑤	⑥	⑦

WRITE ON! Write observations as you rate your week. Note any connections you may see.

_____

_____

_____

_____

SETTING INTENTION. Intention-setting becomes a habit of recognizing what you want (your vision), comparing it against what's real in the present moment (current reality), and closing the gap between the two by taking intentional action in the direction of your vision.

WRITE ON! What are three intentions for this week that will move your current reality closer to your vision?

_____

_____

_____

_____

_____

_____

_____

_____

THREE FEELING WORDS. Feelings change with time and process. Writing is a process that can shift feelings quickly. Before you write, describe your current feeling state in three words or phrases at the top of the page. When your writing is finished, note three feeling words or phrases. Compare the results.

WRITE ON! Try it! Use the prompt, "What's going on?" Time yourself for five minutes. Reflect on any shift in feeling state.

_____

_____

_____

_____

_____

_____

_____

HOW'S YOUR HYDRATION? Are you drinking more water? Establishing a new habit? Falling off? In case you need motivation, try getting a fun new water bottle. Or infuse your water by freezing berries or soft fruit pieces in ice cube trays and using them to chill your drinks. Or drink sparkling water with lime.

WRITE ON! What are three more ways you could drink more water? Get creative.

KEY #3: ATTENTION. How has the quality of your attention been in the last weeks? Before you write, source a scent that you enjoy and that has positive associations for you (e.g., essential oils, soap, coffee beans). Bring it to the write.

WRITE ON! Make a list of everything in the past weeks you have been able to focus full attention on, however briefly. Choose one and describe the experience in a captured moment with sensory detail. Inhale your scent as you write.

_____

_____

_____

_____

_____

_____

_____

_____

_____

_____

_____

_____

_____

_____

_____

_____

_____

_____

_____

_____

_____

_____

MAKING SENSE OF SCENTS. Yesterday you wrote with the help of a scented prop. According to Deborah Ross, L.P.C., pairing an emotionally positive scent with a writing session contributes to the firing and wiring of neural circuitry. The scent needn't be associated with the topic of your writing.

WRITE ON! List scents you love and the positive wash of emotions you associate with them. Then see if you can source these items. Keep them handy for journal time.

WHY WRITING WORKS: STRENGTHEN INTUITION AND INNER GUIDANCE. Your journal becomes a bridge between you and your intuition and inner wisdom. The "still, small voice" becomes clear as we learn to tune in, listen, ask, and act.

WRITE ON! Write about your relationship with intuition and inner wisdom. Has your journal served as a bridge?

_____

_____

_____

_____

_____

_____

_____

WEEKLY REVIEW. Read over the week's entries, reflections, or both. How do you rank your anxiety this week? How do you rank your use of these writing processes? How is the progress of your intentions going? Are you noticing changes?

On a scale of 1 (low) to 7 (high), rate your week:

Anxiety?	1	2	3	4	5	6	7
Writing process?	1	2	3	4	5	6	7
Intentions?	1	2	3	4	5	6	7
Noticing shifts?	1	2	3	4	5	6	7

WRITE ON! Write observations as you rate your week. Note any connections you may see.

_____

_____

_____

_____

_____

SETTING INTENTION. The weekly process of setting intentions brings focus and action orientation to your days. Be sure that your intentions are framed in positive language. Specify what you want rather than what you want to avoid.

WRITE ON! What are three intentions for this week? These can be related to any area of your life. Break larger intentions into week-size bites.

_____

_____

_____

_____

_____

_____

_____

_____

_____

LISTS. Lists are one of the most versatile journal techniques of all. (Do be careful to keep your to-do lists reasonable.) They're great for corralling bits of information and can help us stay mindful.

WRITE ON! Write three lists: "Ten things I'm glad to have in my life." "Five things I'd like to get rid of." "Three awesome things about me." Choose something and write for five minutes.

_____

_____

_____

_____

_____

_____

YOUR ANTI-ANXIETY DIET: ASPARAGUS. According to Dr. Naidoo, asparagus has such outstanding anti-anxiety properties that the Chinese government approved the use of an asparagus extract as a natural functional food and beverage ingredient.

WRITE ON! What's your favorite vegetable? Research its specific food-as-medicine attributes and write what you find. Get curious about the healing (or not) properties of other foods you like.

KEY #4: GENEROSITY. Generosity is often small and simple. A gesture that takes almost no time or effort can be powerful medicine to the recipient. As you develop attention and outlook skills, you'll likely notice organic opportunities to be generous in small and simple ways.

WRITE ON! Set conscious intention in the next week to do three "small and simple" generous acts. Write about the process each time you complete one. What do you notice?

_____

_____

_____

_____

_____

_____

_____

_____

_____

_____

_____

_____

_____

_____

_____

_____

_____

_____

_____

_____

DISCOUNTING THE POSITIVE. In this common cognitive distortion, your mind interprets success as a fluke or somehow not real. For example: Your co-worker tells you she appreciates your contribution to a project. You tell yourself, *"She's just being nice. I didn't do anything special."*

WRITE ON! Do you argue with success? Are you willing to accept success at face value? What can you do differently? Write and reflect.

WHY WRITING WORKS: EXPAND CREATIVITY. It's easy to practice writing a poem or sketching a scene in the journal because it's safe and private. The shedding of inhibitions invites increased flexibility with the creative process, often leading to more creative thinking in behavioral and cognitive change.

WRITE ON! What is your relationship with your creativity? Are you finding that your journal supports the creative process?

_____

_____

_____

_____

_____

_____

_____

WEEKLY REVIEW. Read over the week's entries, reflections, or both. How do you rank your anxiety this week? How do you rank your use of writing? How is the realistic progress of your intentions going? Are you noticing changes?

On a scale of 1 (low) to 7 (high), rate your week:

Anxiety?	①	②	③	④	⑤	⑥	⑦
Writing process?	①	②	③	④	⑤	⑥	⑦
Intentions?	①	②	③	④	⑤	⑥	⑦
Noticing shifts?	①	②	③	④	⑤	⑥	⑦

WRITE ON! Write observations as you rate your week. Note any connections you may see.

_____

_____

_____

SETTING INTENTION. Has your current reality moved closer to your vision in the last week? Every small intention you place attention and take action on closes the gap between current reality and vision.

WRITE ON! What are three intentions for this week?

LIFE BALANCE. Take inventory of various segments of your life to see where you are in and out of balance. Segments typically include physical health, emotional health, family, friends/community, home/environment, work/purpose, finances, and faith/meaning.

WRITE ON! For the less balanced areas, write answers to these questions:
- Where am I now?
- Where do I want to be?
- What are three things I can do, starting now, to gain balance?

Write action steps for each.

_____

_____

_____

_____

_____

_____

_____

EMOTIONAL ACCELERATOR PEDAL. After a sleepless night, brain scans of research participants showed a shutdown of the prefrontal cortex, which normally helps regulate anxiety. Meanwhile, the brains' deeper emotional centers were overactive. "It's almost like the brain is too heavy on the emotional pedal, without enough brake," said co-author Dr. Matthew Walker.

WRITE ON! What's in your mindfulness pantry for quality sleep? Herbal tea? Soft music? Meditation audios? An eye mask? Essential oils? Take inventory.

_____

_____

_____

_____

KEY #1: RESILIENCE. How have you practiced resilience in the last several weeks? What challenges and stresses have you leaned into? How did you manage them?

WRITE ON! Make a list of three to five challenges, stresses, or obstacles you've faced over the last few weeks. What did you do (or not do) that helped you cope? What are you learning about yourself and resilience?

_____

_____

_____

_____

_____

_____

_____

_____

_____

_____

_____

_____

_____

_____

_____

_____

_____

_____

_____

_____

_____

_____

BRAKE PEDAL: SLEEP. In the same study (Day 3), sleep scientist Dr. Eti Ben Simon reported that the deep-sleep study participants experienced a "restoration of the brain mechanism that regulates emotions, lowering reactivity and preventing escalation of anxiety." This can happen every night!

WRITE ON! Keep a paper journal by your bed. Write a bedtime note to your body and brain asking for a night of deep sleep. Pair this with something from your mindfulness pantry.

DATE _____ WEEK 22 • DAY 6

WHY WRITING WORKS: SELF-EMPOWERMENT. Writing encourages self-reliance and personal responsibility. Seeing your life mapped out, one page at a time, makes change observable. It documents the recognition that you are in fact empowering yourself to move toward better-feeling thoughts.

WRITE ON! Write about any shifts toward personal responsibility or self-empowerment in the time you've been working with this journal.

_____

_____

_____

_____

_____

_____

_____

DATE _____ WEEK 22 • DAY 7

WEEKLY REVIEW. Read over the week's entries, reflections, or both. How do you rank your anxiety this week? How do you rank your use of writing? How is the realistic progress of your intentions going? Are you noticing changes?

On a scale of 1 (low) to 7 (high), rate your week:

Anxiety?	① ② ③ ④ ⑤ ⑥ ⑦
Writing process?	① ② ③ ④ ⑤ ⑥ ⑦
Intentions?	① ② ③ ④ ⑤ ⑥ ⑦
Noticing shifts?	① ② ③ ④ ⑤ ⑥ ⑦

WRITE ON! Write observations as you rate your week. Note any connections you may see.

_____

_____

_____

SETTING INTENTION. What's different about your current reality this week? Can you tell that there is movement when intentions are met?

WRITE ON! What are three intentions for this week?

_____

_____

_____

_____

_____

_____

YOUR ANTI-ANXIETY DIET: PROBIOTICS. A recent study suggested a link between foods rich in probiotics (e.g., yogurt, pickles, sauerkraut) and lowered symptoms of social anxiety.

WRITE ON! What if you ate a jar of pickles and suddenly had no social anxiety? Where would you go? Who would you meet? What would you talk about? How would you feel? Might some of that be viable without the pickles?

_____

_____

_____

_____

_____

_____

_____

_____

ALPHAPOEM. This is a poem in which each letter of the alphabet, or of a word or phrase, is written vertically down the page. Each succeeding line begins with a word starting with the next letter—as in, this alphapoem on Worry:

W hat, me worry?
O nly if I forget to
R emember that the
R aggedy old thought can
Y ield to the new, better-feeling thought!

WRITE ON! Unhook your brain. Don't overthink this. Start with Anxiety (Xceptable to cheat for any letters, like X, that might stump you) or Mindfulness down your page. Ready, set go! One minute! Don't think!

KEY #2: OUTLOOK. Are you more able to see the silver linings in the clouds of your past few weeks? Are you being gentle with yourself and others?

WRITE ON! Write a list of times in the past few weeks you've been gentle with yourself or others. Choose at least one story and write it in sensory detail.

_____

_____

_____

_____

_____

_____

_____

_____

_____

_____

_____

_____

_____

_____

_____

_____

_____

_____

_____

_____

_____

_____

NETWORKING MADE EASIER. Networking events and other mingles can spike anxiety even for extroverts. If you've got social anxiety, manage nerves by coming prepared with conversation starters beyond the standard "What do you do?"

WRITE ON! Write some fresh questions for new acquaintances. Examples: "Is there a story behind your first name?" "If you gave a TED Talk, what would it be about?"

WHY WRITING WORKS: CLOSURE WITH THE PAST. Holding on to a past that cannot change is both anxiety producing and energy draining. Resentment, guilt, shame, blame, anger, and hurt are feelings with predictable outcomes. The safe container of your journal allows you to vent, process, and release stored feelings. This closure offers opportunities for forgiveness of yourself and others.

WRITE ON! What in your life are you ready to move on from? What are you ready to release?

_____

_____

_____

_____

_____

_____

WEEKLY REVIEW. Read over the week's entries, reflections, or both. How do you rank your anxiety this week? How do you rank your use of writing? How is the realistic progress of your intentions going? Are you noticing changes?

On a scale of 1 (low) to 7 (high), rate your week:

Anxiety?   ① ② ③ ④ ⑤ ⑥ ⑦

Writing process?   ① ② ③ ④ ⑤ ⑥ ⑦

Intentions?   ① ② ③ ④ ⑤ ⑥ ⑦

Noticing shifts?   ① ② ③ ④ ⑤ ⑥ ⑦

WRITE ON! Write observations as you rate your week. Note any connections you may see.

_____

_____

_____

_____

SETTING INTENTION. Are you remembering to keep your intentions phrased in positive language?

WRITE ON! What are three intentions for this week?

_____

_____

_____

_____

_____

_____

_____

_____

_____

CHARACTER SKETCH. A written portrait of another person, an aspect of yourself, a mood or quality or emotion—versatility is one of the benefits of character sketches. Start with physical descriptions, and then shift to interior qualities, motivations, wishes, desires, and quirks.

WRITE ON! Close your eyes and imagine Anxiety as a person or perhaps a magical being. Observe Anxiety in this form. What does it look like? Wear? Eat for breakfast? What does it want? How does Anxiety get its needs met?

_____

_____

_____

_____

_____

DIAPHRAGMATIC BREATHING. A Chinese research study found that diaphragmatic (deep belly) breathing contributed to healthier states of cognition, emotion, and stress response, including improved cortisol levels. Sustained attention also improved.

WRITE ON! Place your hand on your lower abdomen and take a long, slow, deep breath until your hand rises and your stomach swells. Exhale fully. Continue for eight full breaths. Write notes and observations.

KEY #3: ATTENTION. How is the quality of your focus this week?

WRITE ON! Bullet-list things on your mind. Choose one. Set your phone to airplane mode. Then write, gently disregarding anything that pulls your focus away. Read and reflect.

LET YOUR FREUDIANS SLIP. Sometimes you'll write something you didn't mean to write, and it actually makes sense! Don't fix it! It might be your subconscious mind pushing a message through. Example: "*turning* into" and "*tuning* into" have much different contexts!

WRITE ON! Let's play! Write a worry/anxiety self-talk statement ("I'm no good"). Find a word that you could change just a bit (change or add a letter or two, or change a word to one that sounds similar, such as "I'm so good") that would create a different message.

_____

_____

_____

_____

_____

_____

_____

_____

_____

_____

_____

_____

_____

_____

_____

_____

_____

_____

WHY WRITING WORKS: A WITNESS TO HEALING. Your journal provides an ongoing record of your healing journey. Months and years down the road, you can look back and recognize just how far you've come.

WRITE ON! Who is the healthier self you are becoming?

_____

_____

_____

_____

_____

_____

_____

WEEKLY REVIEW. Read over the week's entries, reflections, or both. How do you rank your anxiety this week? How do you rank your use of writing? How is the realistic progress of your intentions going? Are you noticing changes?

On a scale of 1 (low) to 7 (high), rate your week:

Anxiety?	①	②	③	④	⑤	⑥	⑦
Writing process?	①	②	③	④	⑤	⑥	⑦
Intentions?	①	②	③	④	⑤	⑥	⑦
Noticing shifts?	①	②	③	④	⑤	⑥	⑦

WRITE ON! Write observations as you rate your week. Note any connections you may see.

_____

_____

_____

_____

SETTING INTENTION. It's time to set intentions!

WRITE ON! What are three intentions for this week?

_____

_____

_____

_____

_____

_____

_____

_____

QUESTIONS. While sprints, sentence stems, and other cognitively based journal techniques tend to go forward or backward on a narrative axis, questions drop us down or raise us up on an emotional or philosophical axis. Questions help us explore, probe, layer, examine, and purge.

WRITE ON! Keep a list of questions in your journal. Stay curious and open-ended (e.g., What do I want?) so that you have room to roam in your responses.

_____

_____

_____

_____

_____

_____

_____

A PICTURE SAVES 1,000 WORRIES. Sarah shares her favorite strategy: "I take photos or videos of the actions I used to worry all day about, like locking doors, closing windows, turning off the stove. The photo is proof I don't have to go home and check."

WRITE ON! Write a list of everything you worry about when you leave the house or car. How can you minimize that worry?

KEY #4: GENEROSITY. Think back over the last few weeks. How have you been generous?

WRITE ON! Write about a recent time when you surprised yourself or someone else with a generous action.

_____

_____

_____

_____

_____

_____

_____

_____

_____

_____

_____

_____

_____

_____

_____

_____

_____

_____

_____

_____

_____

_____

_____

ACKNOWLEDGE PROGRESS. Psychologist Dr. Rick Hanson says it's appropriate to recognize that we live in complex, troubled times. There's bad news all around. That's why it's important, he says, to recognize that progress is also happening.

WRITE ON! What is getting better? List ways you moved forward today. They might be small (putting a check in the mail) or large (completing a draft for review). Everything counts. How about progress in the last year? What's different and better?

WHY WRITING WORKS: YOU. The reason writing works for any one person is because that individual has put intention, attention, and action into creating a life made by hand and documented it in the pages or pixels of a journal. If you've come this far, you're likely finding benefits.

WRITE ON! Why is writing working for you? What are you discovering? Which of the reasons are most relevant for you?

_____

_____

_____

_____

_____

_____

_____

WEEKLY REVIEW. Read over the week's entries, reflections, or both. How do you rank your anxiety this week? How do you rank your use of writing? How is the realistic progress of your intentions going? Are you noticing changes?

On a scale of 1 (low) to 7 (high), rate your week:

Anxiety?	1	2	3	4	5	6	7
Writing process?	1	2	3	4	5	6	7
Intentions?	1	2	3	4	5	6	7
Noticing shifts?	1	2	3	4	5	6	7

WRITE ON! Write observations as you rate your week. Note any connections you may see.

_____

_____

_____

_____

INTENTIONS IN REVIEW. In this quarter, you've set intentions for your week. You've been working on breaking big goals or intentions into week-size bites.

WRITE ON! Write about what you've learned from setting intentions each week. Are you evolving as you go, letting yourself learn how to adjust based on experience? Are you discovering what a reasonable weekly goal looks like? Write and reflect.

_____
_____
_____
_____
_____
_____
_____
_____

WRITING IN REVIEW. How have the writing processes and reflection writes contributed to your learning about yourself, anxiety, and mindfulness?

WRITE ON! Which writing techniques and practices have been especially useful? What did you learn or deepen? How about the reflection writes?

_____
_____
_____
_____
_____
_____
_____
_____

SCIENCE IN REVIEW. Which scientific explorations (e.g., neuroscience, research studies) most captured your imagination or determination this quarter?

WRITE ON! Reflect on what you learned or reinforced from the research and science explorations.

_____

_____

_____

_____

_____

_____

_____

_____

_____

_____

_____

_____

_____

_____

_____

_____

_____

_____

_____

_____

_____

KEYS: THE FOUR KEYS IN REVIEW. How have the four keys of well-being (resilience, outlook, attention, generosity) shown up in your life this quarter?

WRITE ON! What is shifting for you in any of these areas of well-being? Are you noticing subtle changes in your thinking or process?

_____

_____

_____

_____

_____

_____

_____

_____

_____

_____

_____

_____

_____

_____

_____

_____

_____

_____

_____

_____

_____

MINDFULNESS IN REVIEW. What do you notice in the area of mindfulness this quarter? What strategies have you learned?

WRITE ON! Reflect on your awareness, attention, and practice of mindfulness techniques learned or reinforced this quarter.

WEEKLY REVIEWS. How well have the weekly reviews helped you observe and track your anxiety, writing, intentions, and outcomes?

WRITE ON! Write about any observations or correlations you have made from Week 13 until now. Reflect on any insights or surprises.

_____

_____

_____

_____

_____

_____

_____

QUARTERLY REVIEW. How do you rank your anxiety for the last 13 weeks? How do you rank your use of these writing processes? How about your intentions? Are you noticing changes?

On a scale of 1 (low) to 7 (high), rate the entire second quarter:

Anxiety?	① ② ③ ④ ⑤ ⑥ ⑦
Writing process?	① ② ③ ④ ⑤ ⑥ ⑦
Intentions?	① ② ③ ④ ⑤ ⑥ ⑦
Noticing shifts?	① ② ③ ④ ⑤ ⑥ ⑦

WRITE ON! Synthesize the past 13 weeks. What have been your major takeaways? Where do you feel as if you're struggling or vulnerable? What have you not yet been able to put into practice? Assess your progress, remembering to be gentle with yourself.

_____

_____

_____

_____

SETTING INTENTION. We're starting a new quarter! Is it time to update some of your intentions?

WRITE ON! Write three intentions for this week, including freshening any old ones.

_____

_____

_____

_____

_____

_____

_____

_____

ANXIETY AS ALLY. It may seem odd to think of anxiety as an ally, but shifting your mindset about anxiety can yield great insight and understanding. The secret? Pay attention. Listen. Let anxiety speak.

WRITE ON! Write down a question you'd like to ask your anxiety, such as, "What do you have to teach me?" Then sit quietly and listen until you sense an answer. Write that down.

_____

_____

_____

_____

_____

_____

_____

_____

UNANIMOUS VERDICT. There is unanimous consensus in anxiety treatment and mindfulness training that taking deep breaths is key. Deep breathing stimulates the parasympathetic (calm-down) response and engages the prefrontal cortex (think-straight) response.

WRITE ON! Engage your focus word from the Relaxation Response from Week 2, Day 5 (your own, or "one") and practice deep breathing for two or three rounds of four breaths. Then write to the question, "What is happening right now?" Reflect.

KEY #1: RESILIENCE. How have you practiced resilience in the last several weeks? What challenges and stresses have you leaned into? How did you manage them?

WRITE ON! Make a list of three to five challenges, stresses, or obstacles you've faced over the last few weeks. What did you do (or not do) that helped you cope? What are you learning about yourself and resilience?

_____

_____

_____

_____

_____

_____

_____

_____

_____

_____

_____

_____

_____

_____

_____

_____

_____

_____

_____

_____

_____

_____

TOUCHBACK: BREATH. Let's practice this again:

B = Box breath or Relaxation Response

R = Roll your shoulders; stretch

E = Extend your clasped hands overhead

A = Adjust your posture (tall and straight)

T = Talk about it, *or*, Tell your journal

H = Hydrate—drink water

WRITE ON! Write about your BREATH experience. Read back and reflect on whether you can consciously practice breathwork every day, even for two or three minutes.

_____

_____

_____

_____

_____

_____

_____

_____

_____

_____

_____

_____

_____

_____

_____

_____

BOLD SELF-CARE. Carol advocates for assertiveness. "Be bold about self-care, no matter what others think. Don't wait for permission to do whatever you need to do."

WRITE ON! Write about the ways, whether obvious or subtle, that you might let your self-care take a backseat to others' approval. Are there people in your life who just don't understand? How can you practice self-advocacy?

_____

_____

_____

_____

_____

_____

_____

WEEKLY REVIEW. Read over the week's entries, reflections, or both. How do you rank your anxiety this week? How do you rank your use of writing? How is the realistic progress of your intentions going? Are you noticing changes?

On a scale of 1 (low) to 7 (high), rate your week:

Anxiety?	①	②	③	④	⑤	⑥	⑦
Writing process?	①	②	③	④	⑤	⑥	⑦
Intentions?	①	②	③	④	⑤	⑥	⑦
Noticing shifts?	①	②	③	④	⑤	⑥	⑦

WRITE ON! Write observations as you rate your week. Note any connections you may see.

_____

_____

_____

_____

SETTING INTENTION. To review the power of intentions: Setting them weekly helps you focus and organize your week around outcomes that really matter to you. Your intentions may include goals or objectives that will help you meet deadlines and stay true to your commitments.

WRITE ON! What are three intentions for this week? Your brain responds better to affirmative language that moves toward what you want instead of away from what you don't want.

_____

_____

_____

_____

_____

_____

_____

BETTER-FEELING THOUGHTS. Remember that when you are feeling anxious or worried, you can reach for a better-feeling thought.

WRITE ON! What are you telling yourself that results in a feeling of worry or anxiety? Write that down. Then name the feeling you would rather be having. Write down a thought that is true and also would produce that feeling. Tell that thought to yourself until the better feeling starts to catch up. Note your observations.

_____

_____

_____

_____

_____

_____

_____

NEGATIVITY BIAS. The brain has a natural bias toward negativity. Way back in the woolly mammoth days, our forebearers were concerned with survival, not quality of life. Our brains still sound the old alarms, but mindfulness practices can help us discern if this alarm reflects a true emergency or whether we can breathe and shift into a calmer state.

WRITE ON! Two columns: On the left, a list of negative thoughts or assumptions that your brain automatically has. On the right, fill in more rational (and better-feeling) thoughts.

KEY #2: OUTLOOK. Are you more able to see the silver linings in the clouds of the past few months? Are you being gentle with yourself and others?

WRITE ON! Write a list of recent times you've been gentle with yourself or others. Choose at least one story and write it in sensory detail. Read and reflect.

POOCH YOUR TUMMY. Shallow or "chest" breathing restricts the diaphragm's range of motion. This lack of air can physiologically contribute to anxious feelings. But as a Harvard Medical School report notes, body image may play a role in keeping breath shallow. Belly breathing requires "pooching out" the tummy, counterintuitive to our flat-stomach culture.

WRITE ON! If you're self-conscious about rounding your belly, write yourself a journal letter from your inner ally encouraging you to breathe deeply.

SOME THOUGHTS CAN'T BE TRUSTED. Kate regains self-regulation in the midst of an anxiety episode with this better-feeling thought: "I'm anxious, so I know I can't trust my thoughts right now."

WRITE ON! Write down some of your untrustworthy thoughts. Write better-feeling thoughts you can tell yourself. If you find yourself repeating thoughts from other writes this week, that's fine. Note it and keep going.

_____

_____

_____

_____

_____

_____

WEEKLY REVIEW. Read over the week's entries, reflections, or both. How do you rank your anxiety this week? How do you rank your use of writing? How is the realistic progress of your intentions going? Are you noticing changes?

On a scale of 1 (low) to 7 (high), rate your week:

Anxiety?	①	②	③	④	⑤	⑥	⑦
Writing process?	①	②	③	④	⑤	⑥	⑦
Intentions?	①	②	③	④	⑤	⑥	⑦
Noticing shifts?	①	②	③	④	⑤	⑥	⑦

WRITE ON! Write observations as you rate your week. Note any connections you may see.

_____

_____

_____

_____

_____

SETTING INTENTION. The weekly process of setting intentions brings focus and action orientation to your days. Remember to use positive language!

WRITE ON! What are three intentions for this week? Are you continuing to review your intentions from the prior week? Celebrate your success!

_____

_____

_____

_____

_____

_____

_____

_____

UNSENT LETTERS. The magic in an unsent letter comes from writing it free from any actual audience. You can speak your truth, in your own voice, in whatever way you wish. It's liberating. Finished? Keep it in your journal, or shred, squash, or burn. (Don't send!)

WRITE ON! Choose someone for your letter. Start, "Dear ___, My heart wants to say . . ." or, "Dear ___, I've been wanting to tell you . . ." Give yourself permission to tell the whole truth faster.

_____

_____

_____

_____

_____

_____

_____

_____

ADRENAL EXHAUSTION. Dr. Bourne notes that anxiety and adrenal exhaustion—a state resulting from protracted stress on the adrenal glands—often co-occur. Adrenal recovery involves lifestyle changes on several fronts: nutrition, relaxation, exercise, even quality sleep.

WRITE ON! If you're susceptible to fight-or-flight responses, take journal inventory of your self-care in these areas. What's already healthy or improving? What needs support?

_____

_____

_____

_____

_____

_____

_____

_____

_____

_____

_____

_____

_____

_____

_____

_____

_____

_____

_____

_____

_____

KEY #3: ATTENTION. Attention is mindfulness in action. Attention keeps you in the present moment. It helps you focus. It helps you process. It supports clear, cohesive thinking.

WRITE ON! Write a list of three to five times in the past week when you have been fully present and paid attention, however briefly. Include sensory details. What do you notice?

_____

_____

_____

_____

_____

_____

_____

_____

_____

_____

_____

_____

_____

_____

_____

_____

_____

_____

_____

_____

_____

_____

FOUR KINDS OF PEACE. When you are at peace, you accept life on life's terms. You're reliably able to find a place of calm. Stress comes and goes; within it, you're able to relax. Dr. Rick Hanson suggests four kinds of peace: the peace of ease, of tranquility, of awareness, and of "what's unchanging."

WRITE ON! When do you experience peace? Which of the four types of peace is most familiar? Which do you long for more of?

PRACTICE: 5–4–3–2–1. Let's review the sensory grounding experience you learned and practiced several months ago (Week 3, Day 5).

WRITE ON! In sensory detail, write five things you see, four things you can touch, three things you hear, two things you smell, one thing you taste. Read back, savor, and reflect. How do you feel?

_____

_____

_____

_____

_____

_____

WEEKLY REVIEW. Read over the week's entries, reflections, or both. How do you rank your anxiety this week? How do you rank your use of writing? How is the realistic progress of your intentions going? Are you noticing changes?

On a scale of 1 (low) to 7 (high), rate your week:

Anxiety?	①	②	③	④	⑤	⑥	⑦
Writing process?	①	②	③	④	⑤	⑥	⑦
Intentions?	①	②	③	④	⑤	⑥	⑦
Noticing shifts?	①	②	③	④	⑤	⑥	⑦

WRITE ON! Write observations as you rate your week. Note any connections you may see.

_____

_____

_____

_____

_____

_____

SETTING INTENTION. The weekly process of setting intentions brings focus and action orientation to your days.

WRITE ON! Write down three intentions for this week.

_____

_____

_____

_____

_____

_____

_____

_____

BEHAVIORAL REHEARSAL. The journal can be a magic time machine in which you transport yourself into a difficult situation and try out different ways to resolve it. In cognitive therapy, this is called a behavioral rehearsal.

WRITE ON! Write a scenario upcoming in the near future that is likely to cause anxiety (e.g., giving a presentation). Starting with the end in mind, write the outcome ("It went really well!") and then several different scenarios of how you got there. (Yes, you are making this up!)

_____

_____

_____

_____

_____

_____

_____

_____

PERFECTLY IMPERFECT. Anne has taught herself to stay away from the rabbit hole of "perfectionistic expectations." Try thinking instead about your day (work performance, parenting, household management) as perfectly imperfect.

WRITE ON! Write about the phrase "perfectly imperfect." What does it suggest? How does it feel? What might it mean to you?

_____

_____

_____

_____

_____

_____

_____

_____

_____

_____

_____

_____

_____

_____

_____

_____

_____

_____

_____

_____

_____

KEY #4: GENEROSITY. Think back over the last few weeks. How have you been generous?

WRITE ON! Make a list of three to five experiences of your own generosity. Choose one and write its story.

_____

_____

_____

_____

_____

_____

_____

_____

_____

_____

_____

_____

_____

_____

_____

_____

_____

_____

_____

_____

_____

_____

_____

_____

_____

PRACTICE: CHARACTER SKETCH. The character sketch technique (Week 24) allows you to personify a feeling or quality as a person or magical being. Take yourself on a creative journey by imagining, for example, the character's wardrobe, soundtrack, desires, motivations, and superpowers. Permission is a key component in anxiety management. Let's get to know Permission!

WRITE ON! Write a character sketch of Permission.

_____

_____

_____

_____

_____

_____

_____

_____

_____

_____

_____

_____

_____

_____

_____

_____

_____

_____

_____

_____

THE PEACE OF EASE. Where are you right now? Are you comfortable and content? Do you have everything you need? Is your breath soft and deep? Is what you gaze upon beautiful or precious, even if (or because of) its state of wear? This is the peace of ease.

WRITE ON! Write about the peace of ease. When do you have it? When does it elude you? What would you need to practice to develop the peace of ease?

_____

_____

_____

_____

_____

_____

_____

WEEKLY REVIEW. Read over the week's entries, reflections, or both. How do you rank your anxiety this week? How do you rank your use of writing? How is the realistic progress of your intentions going? Are you noticing changes?

On a scale of 1 (low) to 7 (high), rate your week:

Anxiety?	①	②	③	④	⑤	⑥	⑦
Writing process?	①	②	③	④	⑤	⑥	⑦
Intentions?	①	②	③	④	⑤	⑥	⑦
Noticing shifts?	①	②	③	④	⑤	⑥	⑦

WRITE ON! Write observations as you rate your week. Note any connections you may see.

_____

_____

_____

_____

_____

SETTING INTENTION. How are your intentions going? Let's set some new or continuing ones!

WRITE ON! What are three intentions for this week? Are there continuing intentions that could use your attention?

_____

_____

_____

_____

_____

_____

_____

_____

CRUMPLE BUTTONS. Do you know your crumple buttons—those vulnerable places that make you feel immediately deflated, weak, or anxious? A principle of neuroplasticity is "name it to tame it." When you can name the triggers that make you crumple, you start the process of taming them.

WRITE ON! What are your crumple buttons? What is your predictable thought pattern when you're triggered? What behavior follows? What would be a better-feeling thought?

_____

_____

_____

_____

_____

THE SPACE BETWEEN. Sarah reminds us, "There is a space between stimulus and response." When you can learn to extend that space, it gives you a chance to consciously choose your response.

WRITE ON! Review yesterday's writing about crumple buttons. Now apply behavioral rehearsal (last week) to imagine ways you can reach that space between stimulus and response.

KEY #1: RESILIENCE. How is your resilience developing?

WRITE ON! What are you noticing about your ability to "fall down and get up" in recent weeks?

_____

_____

_____

_____

_____

_____

_____

_____

_____

_____

_____

_____

_____

_____

_____

_____

_____

_____

_____

_____

_____

_____

RUNNING FOR MIND TRAVEL. Kristen manages her anxiety through running. "When I'm running, I am able to let my mind travel and sort through issues. I also tend to mentally 'write' or feel creative ideas come on."

WRITE ON! Can you try running? How about a long walk in nature? Let your feet and mind both travel. Bring a pocket-size journal and pen so you can make notes about what you see, smell, hear, feel, and think.

_____

_____

_____

_____

_____

_____

_____

_____

_____

_____

_____

_____

_____

_____

_____

_____

_____

_____

_____

PRACTICE: PEACE OF EASE. The peace of ease, you'll recall, is the peace of knowing that everything you have in this moment is everything you need. It is the peace of sufficiency. Practice by paying attention to your senses.

WRITE ON! Practice the 5–4–3–2–1 grounding technique, this time truly focusing on what you see, touch, hear, smell, and taste. Savor each one. Describe it and also describe how it contributes to ease. Read and reflect.

_____

_____

_____

_____

_____

_____

WEEKLY REVIEW. Read over the week's entries, reflections, or both. How do you rank your anxiety this week? How do you rank your use of writing? How is the realistic progress of your intentions going? Are you noticing changes?

On a scale of 1 (low) to 7 (high), rate your week:

Anxiety?	①	②	③	④	⑤	⑥	⑦
Writing process?	①	②	③	④	⑤	⑥	⑦
Intentions?	①	②	③	④	⑤	⑥	⑦
Noticing shifts?	①	②	③	④	⑤	⑥	⑦

WRITE ON! Write observations as you rate your week. Note any connections you may see.

_____

_____

_____

_____

_____

SETTING INTENTION. Time for intentions! Remember to break down larger intentions into week-size portions.

WRITE ON! What are three intentions for this week?

_____

_____

_____

_____

_____

_____

_____

_____

_____

LIFT WEIGHTS, LIFT SPIRITS. A Singapore hospital study found that midlife women with weak upper or lower body strength were more prone to report anxiety symptoms. Maybe feeling strong physically is a remedy for feeling puny emotionally!

WRITE ON! What are simple ways you could improve your physical strength? For instance, you might do bicep curls with a two-pound weight while you talk on the phone. Make a list.

_____

_____

_____

_____

_____

_____

_____

_____

RATIONAL EMOTIVE BEHAVIOR THERAPY. Dr. Albert Ellis, a pioneer in the cognitive therapy movement, created a method in the 1950s called Rational Emotive Behavior Therapy (REBT). He believed that "people are not disturbed by things, but rather by their view of things." In other words, the way people feel is largely influenced by how they think.

WRITE ON! You've been examining your thinking for several months now. How would you synthesize your learning about the relationship between worrisome or anxious thoughts and your emotional state?

_____

_____

_____

_____

_____

_____

_____

_____

_____

_____

_____

_____

_____

_____

_____

_____

_____

KEY #2: OUTLOOK. If you've been mindful about incorporating outlook into your patterns of thinking and behavior, you might be noticing differences by now. Are you seeing shifts?

WRITE ON! What is your current outlook? How do you see the world and those you engage with? Are you noticing differences?

_____

_____

_____

_____

_____

_____

_____

_____

_____

_____

_____

_____

_____

_____

_____

_____

_____

_____

_____

THE PEACE OF AWARENESS. Your mind is chattering, the cramp in your stomach won't leave, the noise is unbearable. The peace of awareness whispers, "*Yes, this is real, and it is okay. You are okay. This is temporary. You are safe, even now, even with this. Just breathe. You are loved.*"

WRITE ON! Write about the peace of awareness. When do you have it? When does it elude you? What would you need to practice to develop the peace of awareness? Read and reflect.

_____

_____

_____

_____

_____

_____

_____

_____

_____

_____

_____

_____

_____

_____

_____

_____

_____

_____

_____

STINKIN' THINKING. Dr. Ellis was legendary for his inventive and often salty language. He called irrational thought processes "stinkin' thinking."

WRITE ON! Today, write Stinkin' Thinking, one letter at a time, down the side of your page. Now write an alphapoem (Week 23) about your own stinkin' thinking, breaking each line when the next line's letter appears. Unhook your brain, write fast, have fun! Reflect.

_____

_____

_____

_____

_____

_____

WEEKLY REVIEW. Read over the week's entries, reflections, or both. How do you rank your anxiety this week? How do you rank your use of writing? How is the realistic progress of your intentions going? Are you noticing changes?

On a scale of 1 (low) to 7 (high), rate your week:

Anxiety?	①	②	③	④	⑤	⑥	⑦
Writing process?	①	②	③	④	⑤	⑥	⑦
Intentions?	①	②	③	④	⑤	⑥	⑦
Noticing shifts?	①	②	③	④	⑤	⑥	⑦

WRITE ON! Write observations as you rate your week. Note any connections you may see.

_____

_____

_____

_____

_____

SETTING INTENTION. Are you making progress on your intentions? About now, you may be noticing that your intentions are building on each other from week to week. This is an excellent way to map progress toward larger goals and intentions.

WRITE ON! What are three intentions for this week?

_____

_____

_____

_____

_____

_____

REBT WORKSHEET. Dr. Ellis, you'll recall from last week, says that feelings follow thoughts. What comes next is a simple yet revolutionary way to change your thoughts into better-feeling ones. First, let's get prepared by sourcing a worksheet on the Internet that will support you in this exploration of Rational Emotive Behavior Therapy.

WRITE ON! Search online for "REBT ABCDE worksheet" to find a choice of templates with instructions and at least one example. Choose one that is identified as coming from a trained REBT therapist or treatment center. Print several copies. Set aside for a later assignment. Write about a recent situation when you were feeling fine until something happened that upset you and changed your mood completely.

_____

_____

_____

_____

_____

_____

THE ABC OF REBT. Now let's start in! Locate your REBT worksheet and use it as we proceed. A is for Activating Event. You're on the freeway and a car cuts in front of you to get to the exit ramp. B is for Belief. You immediately think: "That jerk almost killed me!" C is for Consequence. You feel panic, rage, or fear. (You also likely had an adrenaline surge.)

WRITE ON! Starting with your scenario from yesterday, write out two or three more of your own recent upsets, identifying the stages as A, B, and C. This lesson continues throughout this week.

_____

_____

_____

_____

_____

_____

_____

_____

_____

_____

_____

_____

_____

_____

_____

_____

_____

_____

_____

_____

_____

KEY #3: ATTENTION. In her poem "Prospective Immigrants Please Note," Adrienne Rich writes, "Things look at you doubly/and you must look back/and let them happen." This too is attention.

WRITE ON! What has "looked at you doubly" in the last few weeks? What has captured your attention that you looked back at, even though you might not have wanted to?

WHAT IS RATIONAL? *Rational*, as Dr. Ellis uses the word, means real, actual, evidence-based, data-driven, verifiable, observably true. The test question: "Is there any rational evidence to support the truth of B (my Belief)?"

WRITE ON! Check it out in your scenarios from Day 3. Is there any rational evidence to support the truth of your Belief? It's likely there won't be, but more about that tomorrow.

THE D OF REBT. Earlier, you made meaning—"a jerk almost killed me"—from a careless highway lane change. The D in REBT is Disputing. It starts with the rational evidence question and, in this case, there's no evidence to support that you were harmed. D continues with Disputing the original Belief.

WRITE ON! Go back to your scenarios and dispute your original beliefs. What is rationally true? In our example, it is verifiable and observable that a driver used poor judgment and crossed your path in an inappropriate way, and your pulse rate validates that you were in fight-or-flight mode.

_____

_____

_____

_____

_____

_____

WEEKLY REVIEW. Read over the week's entries, reflections, or both. How do you rank your anxiety this week? How do you rank your use of writing? How is the realistic progress of your intentions going? Are you noticing changes?

On a scale of 1 (low) to 7 (high), rate your week:

Anxiety?	①	②	③	④	⑤	⑥	⑦
Writing process?	①	②	③	④	⑤	⑥	⑦
Intentions?	①	②	③	④	⑤	⑥	⑦
Noticing shifts?	①	②	③	④	⑤	⑥	⑦

WRITE ON! Write observations as you rate your week. Note any connections you may see.

_____

_____

_____

_____

SETTING INTENTION. Time for intentions!

WRITE ON! What are three intentions for this week? Maybe there's a new area of your life that would like an intention and some attention?

_____

_____

_____

_____

_____

_____

_____

THE E OF REBT. Lastly, we have the E, for Effective New Emotion. If the meaning you make from this close call is that the driver used poor judgment and gave you quite a scare, then what is the effective new emotion? You still get an adrenaline rush, but your feeling is likely to be more like righteous indignation, not rage.

WRITE ON! Finish out your own example. Then read everything together and reflect.

_____

_____

_____

_____

_____

_____

_____

_____

THE PEACE OF TRANQUILITY. This peace is the leaf falling into the perfectly still lake. It is the deep quiet of freshly fallen snow. "Except for the point, the still point/there can be no dance," wrote T.S. Eliot. The peace of tranquility is the still point.

WRITE ON! Write about the peace of tranquility. When do you have it? When does it elude you? What would you need to practice to develop the peace of tranquility? Read and reflect.

_____

_____

_____

_____

_____

_____

_____

_____

_____

_____

_____

_____

_____

_____

_____

_____

_____

_____

_____

KEY #4: GENEROSITY. Generosity includes generosity to self. Generosity to self can include forgiveness for mistakes, play dates with family or friends, fresh air and sunshine, naps, time for breathwork, patience, and so much more.

WRITE ON! How are you generous to yourself? Make a list of three to five ways you have been self-generous over the past few weeks. Read and reflect.

_____

_____

_____

_____

_____

_____

_____

_____

_____

_____

_____

_____

_____

_____

_____

_____

_____

_____

_____

_____

LOVING YOURSELF. Alex offers his touchstone for self-calm: "I just repeat to myself, 'I love you.'"

WRITE ON! On your page or screen, write "[Your name], I love you." Sit for a moment and gaze at those words. What arises? Write it down. Repeat until you can embrace self-love. (This might take several tries.) Accept this as an act of generosity to self.

ANXIETY INTO MUSCLE. Catherine finds strength training to be a consistent touchstone. "It takes that anxious energy and transforms it into muscle by pushing and lifting weights."

WRITE ON! Write about a time when you felt empowered by exercise. If you've ever done (or now do) strength training, write about how it feels to be strong.

_____

_____

_____

_____

_____

_____

_____

WEEKLY REVIEW. Read over the week's entries, reflections, or both. How do you rank your anxiety this week? How do you rank your use of writing? How is the realistic progress of your intentions going? Are you noticing changes?

On a scale of 1 (low) to 7 (high), rate your week:

Anxiety?	①	②	③	④	⑤	⑥	⑦
Writing process?	①	②	③	④	⑤	⑥	⑦
Intentions?	①	②	③	④	⑤	⑥	⑦
Noticing shifts?	①	②	③	④	⑤	⑥	⑦

WRITE ON! Write observations as you rate your week. Note any connections you may see.

_____

_____

_____

_____

_____

SETTING INTENTION. What have you been procrastinating about? This week, see if there are three things you could knock off your perpetual to-do list by setting them as intentions.

WRITE ON! Write three intentions this week, including one or more tasks you've been putting off.

_____

_____

_____

_____

_____

_____

_____

_____

SELF-COMPASSION. Becoming mindful about anxiety means we must learn to treat ourselves with the same compassion we would extend to a hungry child or a homeless family. Self-compassion expert Dr. Kristen Neff suggests self-talk such as, "This is really difficult right now. How can I care for and comfort myself in this moment?"

WRITE ON! In your journal, ask the question, "How can I care for and comfort myself?" Let yourself respond. This may go on for several rounds.

_____

_____

_____

_____

_____

_____

_____

_____

A SILENT MOMENT. Lorenzo has a simple, profound touchstone for self-regulation: "Go into a room for a silent moment."

WRITE ON! Do you have a self-care sanctuary, bedroom, basement, bathroom, or closet you can slip into for a few minutes of silence and breathing? If so, write about how it serves you. If not, write about how you might carve out a space to take silent moments.

KEY #1: RESILIENCE. How have you practiced resilience in the last several weeks? What challenges and stresses have you leaned into? How did you manage them?

WRITE ON! Make a list of three to five challenges, stresses, or obstacles you've faced over the last few weeks. What did you do (or not do) that helped you cope? What are you learning about yourself and resilience?

_____

_____

_____

_____

_____

_____

_____

_____

_____

_____

_____

_____

_____

_____

_____

_____

_____

_____

_____

_____

_____

_____

PRACTICE: PEACE OF AWARENESS. This is the peace of mindful focus and compassionate acceptance. Practice with your self-talk. Allow yourself to hold both the awareness of your immediate reality (panic, worry, agitation) and your capacity to soothe yourself with a larger context of loving-kindness.

PASSING PAIN. Lynn offers this ironic Ten-Word Tip: "This too shall pass. Maybe like a kidney stone, though!"

WRITE ON! Bring to mind a time that was very painful and then passed. What were the strengths and resources, inner and outer, that you drew upon to sustain yourself?

_____

_____

_____

_____

_____

_____

WEEKLY REVIEW. Read over the week's entries, reflections, or both. How do you rank your anxiety this week? How do you rank your use of writing? How is the realistic progress of your intentions going? Are you noticing changes?

On a scale of 1 (low) to 7 (high), rate your week:

Anxiety?	①	②	③	④	⑤	⑥	⑦
Writing process?	①	②	③	④	⑤	⑥	⑦
Intentions?	①	②	③	④	⑤	⑥	⑦
Noticing shifts?	①	②	③	④	⑤	⑥	⑦

WRITE ON! Write observations as you rate your week. Note any connections you may see.

_____

_____

_____

_____

_____

_____

SETTING INTENTION. Are there intentions from weeks ago that might benefit from a check-in or touchback?

WRITE ON! Write three intentions for this week, perhaps refreshing prior intentions that could use a boost.

_____

_____

_____

_____

_____

_____

_____

DIALOGUE. The classic journal dialogue comes from the work of Dr. Ira Progoff. A journal dialogue is a written conversation in which you write both parts. On the page, it looks like a play script. It requires willingness to temporarily suspend disbelief and engage in the invention of another's thoughts and feelings. Still, it's often surprisingly powerful.

WRITE ON! Choose a dialogue partner, which can be an actual person or an abstraction, like Anxiety or Mindfulness. Imagine you are together in a beautiful place in nature. Have a productive, respectful conversation, asking and answering in turn. Stay friendly.

_____

_____

_____

_____

_____

_____

_____

RELAX YOUR TONGUE. Zen Master Thích Thông Triêt, creator of the Sunyata meditation method, which blends four Buddhist traditions with neuroscience, says relaxing the tongue "results in a quiet mind in which there are no wandering or anxious thoughts."

WRITE ON! Try it. Sit comfortably upright and breathe deeply. Relax your tongue. Internally repeat _"I am relaxing my tongue."_ Stay there for three to seven minutes. Pay attention to your body and your thoughts. Write your discoveries.

KEY #2: OUTLOOK. Are you more able to see the silver linings in the clouds of your past few weeks? Are you being gentle with yourself and others?

WRITE ON! Write a list of times in the past few weeks you've been gentle with yourself or others. Choose at least one story and write it in sensory detail. Read and reflect.

_____

_____

_____

_____

_____

_____

_____

_____

_____

_____

_____

_____

_____

_____

_____

_____

_____

_____

_____

_____

_____

_____

_____

ACCEPT DIFFICULTY. Psychologist Dr. Hanson encourages the acknowledgment that life is filled with challenges. When we resist or worry, that only compounds stress. Instead, acknowledge that you're worried, stressed, fatigued. Tell yourself, *"This is difficult. It's okay that it feels difficult."*

WRITE ON! Bring to mind a current situation that is hard. Describe it briefly, then write the two sentences from above. Continue writing, staying open to surprises. Pay attention to any release you may experience.

MOVEMENT MEDITATIONS. Movement meditations such as yoga, tai chi, or qigong can be useful in centering, in grounding, and even in releasing endorphins. Mary describes her touchstone: "Qigong opens up the body's energy meridians, allowing positive healing energy to flow. It is also a distraction to whatever is causing my anxiety."

WRITE ON! Write about a time you found relief or peace of mind in movement.

_____

_____

_____

_____

_____

_____

_____

WEEKLY REVIEW. Read over the week's entries, reflections, or both. How do you rank your anxiety this week? How do you rank your use of writing? How is the realistic progress of your intentions going? Are you noticing changes?

On a scale of 1 (low) to 7 (high), rate your week:

Anxiety?	1	2	3	4	5	6	7
Writing process?	1	2	3	4	5	6	7
Intentions?	1	2	3	4	5	6	7
Noticing shifts?	1	2	3	4	5	6	7

WRITE ON! Write observations as you rate your week. Note any connections you may see.

_____

_____

_____

_____

_____

SETTING INTENTION. This week, you might think about intentions around anything you've been procrastinating on, shoving to the bottom of the list, or otherwise not finding time or attention for.

WRITE ON! See if you can include an intention about something you've been setting aside for a while.

_____

_____

_____

_____

_____

_____

_____

_____

THE PACE OF GUIDANCE. Journal therapy pioneer Christina Baldwin suggests we "move at the pace of guidance."

WRITE ON! Sit quietly with your journal on your lap or your keyboard handy. Breathe deeply and center yourself. Passively disregard any thoughts. Imagine yourself on an open path of your choice, moving at the pace of your traveling companion, Guidance. Guidance offers wisdom. Write whatever you hear, feel, or sense.

_____

_____

_____

_____

_____

_____

_____

FOREST BATHING. Forest bathing, known as shinrin-yoku in Japan, has received increasing attention in recent years for its positive effects on human health. A study from China correlates reduction in inflammation and cortisol levels with the experience of walking slowly in a quiet, forested area.

WRITE ON! Take your mind for a walk in a beautiful place in nature—forest, park, lakeside, shore, garden. Release your stress to the elements. Bring your journal to document observations.

KEY #3: ATTENTION. How is the quality of your attention of late? Where do you place your attention? What do you notice?

WRITE ON! Write a list of three to five times in the past week or two when you have paid mindful attention. Is there anything you did not pay attention to that you later regretted? If so, list that as well. Write for five minutes about anything on your list. Read and reflect.

_____

_____

_____

_____

_____

_____

_____

_____

_____

_____

_____

_____

_____

_____

_____

_____

_____

_____

_____

_____

_____

_____

_____

_____

THE PEACE OF WHAT'S UNCHANGING. The sun dawns, the moon rises, dusk falls. The peace of what's unchanging grounds you and reminds you that every changing moment, you are cradled by a large and generous universe.

WRITE ON! Write about the peace of what's unchanging. When do you have it? When does it elude you? What would you need to practice to develop this peace?

_____

_____

_____

_____

_____

_____

_____

_____

_____

_____

_____

_____

_____

_____

_____

_____

_____

_____

_____

_____

_____

NEVER ALONE. Mary lives by the wisdom offered to her by a spiritual teacher: "You are never alone. God is always with you."

WRITE ON! Write about that which comforts, sustains, or is constantly present for you in a benevolent or protective way, whether deity, universal principle, or humanist value.

_____

_____

_____

_____

_____

_____

WEEKLY REVIEW. Read over the week's entries, reflections, or both. How do you rank your anxiety this week? How do you rank your use of writing? How is the realistic progress of your intentions going? Are you noticing changes?

On a scale of 1 (low) to 7 (high), rate your week:

Anxiety?	①	②	③	④	⑤	⑥	⑦
Writing process?	①	②	③	④	⑤	⑥	⑦
Intentions?	①	②	③	④	⑤	⑥	⑦
Noticing shifts?	①	②	③	④	⑤	⑥	⑦

WRITE ON! Write observations as you rate your week. Note any connections you may see.

_____

_____

_____

_____

_____

SETTING INTENTION. Time to set intentions for the week!

WRITE ON! This week, how about setting at least one intention to treat yourself with something fun or relaxing?

_____

_____

_____

_____

_____

_____

MENTOR POEMS. Poetry therapy offers the concept of a "mentor poem," a poem that teaches, soothes, or companions you. Do you have a favorite poem from any time in your life? It can also be a song lyric, sacred text, Psalm, or prayer. The most important quality is that it inspires, soothes, or teaches you.

WRITE ON! Write or print this piece by hand. Or, if writing digitally, place it in color or a special font. Love the words as you write them. Take them into your body. Notice where they land. Write your experience and reflect.

_____

_____

_____

_____

_____

_____

_____

_____

PRACTICE: PEACE OF WHAT'S UNCHANGING. This is the peace of stability, of groundedness. Practice by being in nature. Whatever the weather, whatever season it is, go outside. Feel the earth—a rock, a leaf, the dirt. Feel the air—a breeze, the rain, the heat. Observe the beauty—arid, frozen, lush.

WRITE ON! Take a nature walk (your own street works just fine) and pay attention to the natural elements of earth, air, water, and fire; animal, vegetable, mineral. Write, read, reflect.

KEY #4: GENEROSITY. Think back over the last few weeks. How have you been generous?

WRITE ON! Make a list of three to five experiences of your own generosity. Be sure to include times when you were generous with yourself. Choose one and write its story. Read and reflect.

_____

_____

_____

_____

_____

_____

_____

_____

_____

_____

_____

_____

_____

_____

_____

_____

_____

_____

_____

_____

_____

_____

SOOTHING WORDS. Kitty, a poet and lover of poetry, invokes the mentor poem concept with her Ten-Word Tip: "Learn your favorite poems by heart. Silently recite when needed."

WRITE ON! Learn some of the lines of your mentor poem (Day 2) by heart. Silently recite when needed.

THE YOGA CURE. A psychiatric study from Boston University correlates consistent yoga practice for as little as one month with significant improvement in sleep quality, tranquility, and positivity, and the decrease in physical exhaustion and symptoms of both anxiety and depression.

WRITE ON! Write about your history with yoga, stretching, dance, athletics—anything that stretches your muscles and calms your mind. Choose a story from your history and tell it (or tell the story of having no history).

_____

_____

_____

_____

_____

WEEKLY REVIEW. Read over the week's entries, reflections, or both. How do you rank your anxiety this week? How do you rank your use of writing? How is the realistic progress of your intentions going? Are you noticing changes?

On a scale of 1 (low) to 7 (high), rate your week:

Anxiety?	①	②	③	④	⑤	⑥	⑦
Writing process?	①	②	③	④	⑤	⑥	⑦
Intentions?	①	②	③	④	⑤	⑥	⑦
Noticing shifts?	①	②	③	④	⑤	⑥	⑦

WRITE ON! Write observations as you rate your week. Note any connections you may see.

_____

_____

_____

_____

INTENTIONS IN REVIEW. In this quarter, you've set intentions for your week. You've been working on breaking big goals or intentions into week-size bites.

WRITE ON! Write about what you've learned from setting intentions each week. Are you evolving as you go, letting yourself learn how to adjust based on experience? Are you discovering what a reasonable weekly goal looks like? Write and reflect.

_____

_____

_____

_____

_____

_____

_____

_____

WRITING IN REVIEW. How have the writing processes and reflection writes contributed to your learning about yourself, anxiety, and mindfulness?

WRITE ON! Which writing techniques and practices have been especially useful? What did you learn or deepen? How about the reflection writes?

_____

_____

_____

_____

_____

_____

_____

_____

_____

SCIENCE IN REVIEW. Which scientific explorations most captured your imagination or determination this quarter?

WRITE ON! Reflect on what you learned or reinforced from the research and science explorations.

_____

_____

_____

_____

_____

_____

_____

_____

_____

_____

_____

_____

_____

_____

_____

_____

_____

_____

_____

_____

KEYS: THE FOUR KEYS IN REVIEW. How have the four keys of well-being (resilience, out-look, attention, generosity) shown up in your life this quarter?

WRITE ON! What is shifting for you in any of these areas of well-being? Are you noticing shifts in your thinking or process? Write and reflect.

_____

_____

_____

_____

_____

_____

_____

_____

_____

_____

_____

_____

_____

_____

_____

_____

_____

_____

_____

_____

_____

MINDFULNESS IN REVIEW. What do you notice in the area of mindfulness this quarter? What strategies have you learned, practiced, and deepened?

WRITE ON! Reflect on your awareness, attention, and practice of mindfulness techniques learned or reinforced this quarter.

_____

_____

_____

_____

_____

_____

_____

_____

_____

_____

_____

_____

_____

_____

_____

_____

_____

_____

_____

_____

_____

WEEKLY REVIEWS. How well have the weekly reviews helped you observe and track your anxiety, writing, intentions, and outcomes?

WRITE ON! Write about any observations or correlations you have made. Reflect on any insights or surprises.

_____

_____

_____

_____

_____

_____

QUARTERLY REVIEW. How do you rank your anxiety for the last 13 weeks? How do you rank your use of these writing processes? How about your intentions? Mindfulness? Are you noticing changes?

On a scale of 1 (low) to 7 (high), rate the entire third quarter:

Anxiety?	①	②	③	④	⑤	⑥	⑦
Writing process?	①	②	③	④	⑤	⑥	⑦
Intentions?	①	②	③	④	⑤	⑥	⑦
Noticing shifts?	①	②	③	④	⑤	⑥	⑦

WRITE ON! Synthesize the past 13 weeks. What have been your major takeaways? Where do you feel as if you're struggling or vulnerable? What have you not yet been able to put into practice? Assess your progress, remembering to be gentle with yourself.

_____

_____

_____

_____

SETTING INTENTION. What would you like to create this week? Keep your language positive.

WRITE ON! What are three intentions for this week? Keep them week-size. Progress, not perfection!

_____

_____

_____

_____

_____

_____

_____

PERSPECTIVES: TIME. The journal technique of perspectives alters point of view, either through shifting time (most commonly, writing into the future) or voice (most commonly, writing your own story in the third person).

WRITE ON! Date your page six months from today. Imagine that you have continued to bring writing and mindfulness toolbox skills to soothe anxiety. Who will you be? Write in first person, present tense ("I am").

_____

_____

_____

_____

_____

_____

_____

SELF-KINDNESS. Dr. Neff (Week 35, Day 2) identifies self-kindness as a key element in self-compassion. Self-kindness means that you don't expect yourself to be perfect. You know you're a work in progress, and you tolerate setbacks without self-blame. Self-judgment recedes to the background as you commit to the practice of self-kindness.

WRITE ON! Write about a time when you were caught up in self-judgment. Write a second story about a time when you treated yourself with self-kindness.

_____

_____

_____

_____

_____

_____

_____

_____

_____

_____

_____

_____

_____

_____

_____

_____

_____

_____

KEY #1: RESILIENCE. How have you managed challenges in the past several weeks?

WRITE ON! Check in with resilience skills and strategies. How are you falling down? How are you getting up?

_____

_____

_____

_____

_____

_____

_____

_____

_____

_____

_____

_____

_____

_____

_____

_____

_____

_____

_____

_____

_____

PERFECTION OPTIONAL. Mitch considers perfection to be overrated. "Forget about doing 100 percent. Just do 50 percent. Doing something is better than doing nothing at all."

WRITE ON! How do you begin? What do you need to get started? Write about how you initiate action. Are there adjustments that would serve you?

_____

_____

_____

_____

_____

_____

_____

_____

_____

_____

_____

_____

_____

_____

_____

_____

_____

_____

_____

A BRISK WALK. According to the Anxiety and Depression Association of America, a 10-minute walk may help manage moods surprisingly well. AADA compares a brisk walk or other simple activity to taking an aspirin for a headache—it can deliver several hours of relief.

WRITE ON! Write three feeling words before you head out for a 10- to 15-minute walk. Focus on the sensory experience. Write three feeling words when you return.

_____

_____

_____

_____

_____

_____

WEEKLY REVIEW. Read over the week's entries, reflections, or both. How do you rank your anxiety this week? How do you rank your use of writing? How is the realistic progress of your intentions going? Are you noticing changes?

On a scale of 1 (low) to 7 (high), rate your week:

Anxiety?	① ② ③ ④ ⑤ ⑥ ⑦
Writing process?	① ② ③ ④ ⑤ ⑥ ⑦
Intentions?	① ② ③ ④ ⑤ ⑥ ⑦
Noticing shifts?	① ② ③ ④ ⑤ ⑥ ⑦

WRITE ON! Write observations as you rate your week. Note any connections you may see.

_____

_____

_____

_____

_____

SETTING INTENTION. It's intention time! Think ahead to what you'd like to have completed or advanced this week.

WRITE ON! What are three intentions for this week? Keep them week-size. Progress, not perfection!

_____

_____

_____

_____

_____

_____

_____

PERSPECTIVES: VOICE. Last week, we shifted time. Today, we'll shift voice. Write your own story in the third person. This provides you with useful detachment, and you can get a broader perspective.

WRITE ON! Bring to mind a recent moment of embarrassment, nervousness, annoyance, or other mild negative emotion. Place yourself in that scene. Now, as if you are watching a movie play out, write this character's experience in the third-person voice of a compassionate witness.

_____

_____

_____

_____

_____

_____

_____

"WEIGHTLESS" SOUND THERAPY. A UK neuroscience team has discovered the number-one song in the world for reducing anxiety. Composed in conjunction with sound therapists, the song reduced overall anxiety in research participants by a remarkable 65 percent.

WRITE ON! YouTube has both 8-minute and 10-hour versions of "Weightless" by Marconi Union. Choose a current nagging issue or anxiety, pop in your earbuds, and write for the duration of the eight-minute instrumental. Reflect.

KEY #2: OUTLOOK. How is your outlook? Check out things like whether you're able to assume positive intent or look for the possible good in a challenge. Perhaps you're having better-feeling thoughts.

WRITE ON! Check in with yourself. Read back and reflect. Do you see any patterns that have emerged?

_____

_____

_____

_____

_____

_____

_____

_____

_____

_____

_____

_____

_____

_____

_____

_____

_____

_____

_____

_____

_____

_____

NOBODY ELSE KNOWS, EITHER. Another element of self-compassion is recognizing that we are not the only frail humans who don't know what we're doing. Nobody else knows, either. We're all figuring it out as we go. Everyone feels inadequate some of the time. Self-compassion recognizes that "suffering and personal inadequacy are part of the shared human experience."

WRITE ON! Write a story about a time when you felt isolated and alone. Write another story about a time when you felt connected to and a part of the shared human experience.

_____

_____

_____

_____

_____

_____

_____

_____

_____

_____

_____

_____

_____

_____

_____

_____

_____

_____

_____

_____

BENEFITS OF EXERCISE. Some benefits of regular exercise include sharper memory and thinking, increased self-esteem, better sleep, more energy, stronger resilience, and better coping skills. What are you waiting for? Lace up those sneakers!

WRITE ON! Which of these benefits are most appealing to you? Try tracking your walks, cardio, strength training, or meditative movement through the lens of one or two of these outcomes. What do you notice?

_____

_____

_____

_____

_____

_____

WEEKLY REVIEW. Read over the week's entries, reflections, or both. How do you rank your anxiety this week? How do you rank your use of writing? How is the realistic progress of your intentions going? Are you noticing changes?

On a scale of 1 (low) to 7 (high), rate your week:

Anxiety?	① ② ③ ④ ⑤ ⑥ ⑦
Writing process?	① ② ③ ④ ⑤ ⑥ ⑦
Intentions?	① ② ③ ④ ⑤ ⑥ ⑦
Noticing shifts?	① ② ③ ④ ⑤ ⑥ ⑦

WRITE ON! Write observations as you rate your week. Note any connections you may see.

_____

_____

_____

_____

_____

SETTING INTENTION. How are your intentions coming along? Are there carry-forwards from the last week or two that you'd like to wrap up?

WRITE ON! Write your three intentions this week. Is there anything you can bring closure to?

STEPPING STONES LIST. Dr. Progoff developed an approach using "stepping stones," a list of the turning points of your life. These are events and experiences that changed you and continue to impact your life as you are living it today.

WRITE ON! Make a list of 10 to 15 life events from birth to the present moment that changed and shaped you. Write the list in the form of short paragraphs. We'll continue along with this next week.

HAPPINESS HABITS: 40%. Social psychologist Dr. Sonja Lyubomirsky studies happiness. She finds that genetically determined set points account for about 50 percent of one's capacity for happiness. Only 10 percent is ascribed to circumstances (e.g., being rich/poor, sick/healthy). The other 40 percent? Thoughts and actions! How we think and what we do account for nearly half of our potential happiness.

WRITE ON! Write about a time when you were happy. Reconstruct the thoughts you were thinking, the emotions you were feeling, what you were doing. If you need to make it up (retrospectively re-create it), that's poetic truth, and it's fine.

_____

_____

_____

_____

_____

_____

_____

_____

_____

_____

_____

_____

_____

_____

_____

_____

_____

KEY #3: ATTENTION. To what are you paying attention in recent weeks?

WRITE ON! Check in with yourself on your attention.

_____

_____

_____

_____

_____

_____

_____

_____

_____

HOW'S YOUR MINDFULNESS PANTRY? Let's inventory your mindfulness pantry. What resources, tools, shortcuts, and methods do you have on hand? Does anything need to be refreshed? Do you have any new resources or tools to add?

WRITE ON! Take inventory of your mindfulness pantry. What are you using most these days? What is past its prime and maybe needs updating?

_____

_____

_____

_____

_____

_____

_____

LOWER YOUR STANDARDS. The poet William Stafford was known for writing a new poem every day. Admirers often asked how they, too, could develop the discipline of writing a poem a day. Stafford's wry reply: "Lower your standards."

WRITE ON! What's something you'd like to have more of in your life—exercise, healthy foods, time to write? What if you lowered your standards and accepted less than ideal circumstances to get started?

_____

_____

_____

_____

_____

_____

WEEKLY REVIEW. Read over the week's entries, reflections, or both. How do you rank your anxiety this week? How do you rank your use of writing? How is the realistic progress of your intentions going? Are you noticing changes?

On a scale of 1 (low) to 7 (high), rate your week:

Anxiety?	①	②	③	④	⑤	⑥	⑦
Writing process?	①	②	③	④	⑤	⑥	⑦
Intentions?	①	②	③	④	⑤	⑥	⑦
Noticing shifts?	①	②	③	④	⑤	⑥	⑦

WRITE ON! Write observations as you rate your week. Note any connections you may see.

_____

_____

_____

_____

_____

DATE _____   **W**EEK **43** • **D**AY **1**

SETTING INTENTION. What would you like to create this week? Keep your language positive.

WRITE ON! What are three intentions for this week?

_____

_____

_____

_____

_____

_____

_____

_____

DATE _____   **W**EEK **43** • **D**AY **2**

STEPPING STONES STORY. The work of stepping stones (Week 42, Day 2) is enhanced with distance, so set aside any on your list that are happening currently or were resolved only recently. From the others, choose one that draws your attention or moves you in a particular way. Perhaps your stepping stone will choose you. If so, accept it.

WRITE ON! Set your timer for 20 minutes. Center yourself with breath and bring to mind the stepping stone. Note how one phrase, like "cancer diagnosis," captures a whole span of time. Begin with Dr. Progoff's ritual phrase, *"It was a time when . . ."*

_____

_____

_____

_____

_____

_____

_____

HAPPINESS HABIT #1: GRATITUDE. Dr. Lyubomirsky says that gratitude is a metastrategy for happiness, as it helps us savor life's experiences, encourages ethical behavior, and helps deal with stress and trauma. Also, gratitude tends to neutralize negative feelings.

WRITE ON! On scraps of paper, write the names of 10 people you love or hold in high regard. Fold them up and put them in a bowl. Draw one and write a letter to that person expressing gratitude. You can deliver it if you wish, but just the writing produces positive effects. Repeat as desired.

KEY #4: GENEROSITY. How is your generosity of heart, mind, body, money, and service these last weeks? Who is being generous to you? Are you generous with yourself?

WRITE ON! Check in on your generosity experiences and takeaways from the last few weeks.

_____

_____

_____

_____

_____

_____

_____

_____

_____

_____

_____

_____

_____

_____

_____

_____

_____

_____

_____

_____

_____

_____

_____

_____

_____

AROUSING FROM SLEEP. A stepping-stone story is an initiation. It arouses from sleep potent seeds of insight, inspiration, or integration that were planted during the initial experience, and perhaps now can come forward as fresh discoveries. Water these seeds.

WRITE ON! Write about who you were then and who you are now. What do you want to say to your younger self? Is there anything that was activated at that age that resonates with life as you're living it today?

_____

_____

_____

_____

_____

_____

_____

_____

_____

_____

_____

_____

_____

_____

_____

_____

_____

_____

_____

_____

_____

_____

_____

A MINDFUL TRUCE. William Stafford's son Kim, a medieval scholar, has another take on his father's "lower your standards" quip. When armies fought in the Middle Ages, the standard-bearers took the field, flags waving, signaling readiness for battle. Conversely, if the commanders wanted truce, the standard-bearer rode out with a lowered flag—a lowered standard.

WRITE ON! Where do you feel at war with yourself? What if you were to take a mindful pause—a truce—by lowering the flag of internal conflict and allowing mindful observation?

_____

_____

_____

_____

_____

_____

WEEKLY REVIEW. Read over the week's entries, reflections, or both. How do you rank your anxiety this week? How do you rank your use of writing? How is the realistic progress of your intentions going? Are you noticing changes?

On a scale of 1 (low) to 7 (high), rate your week:

Anxiety?	①	②	③	④	⑤	⑥	⑦
Writing process?	①	②	③	④	⑤	⑥	⑦
Intentions?	①	②	③	④	⑤	⑥	⑦
Noticing shifts?	①	②	③	④	⑤	⑥	⑦

WRITE ON! Write observations as you rate your week. Note any connections you may see.

_____

_____

_____

_____

SETTING INTENTION. Remember that intention-setting becomes a habit of recognizing what you want (your vision), comparing it against what's real in the present moment (current reality), and closing the gap between the two by taking intentional action in the direction of your vision.

WRITE ON! What are three intentions for this week that will help advance your current reality in the direction of your vision?

_____

_____

_____

_____

_____

_____

_____

ART MAKING. Simple art making in the journal is easy and fun. Start with crayons, colored pencils, and glue sticks. Add accoutrements like stickers and washi tape, if you wish. Sketch, draw, doodle, color, collage. Have fun!

WRITE ON! Capture your current state of mood, mind, or mindfulness in color, shape, or form. Or make a small collage in your journal with words, phrases, and images from old magazines. Give your picture a title. Hang it up!

_____

_____

_____

_____

_____

_____

_____

_____

HAPPINESS HABIT #2: SAVORING PLEASURE. Brain science shows that neural circuitry can be recruited and installed through savoring—letting a positive sensory experience deepen as it is relished. People who hang on to the good in life and savor happy memories are better able to buffer stress.

WRITE ON! Find an experience to savor—a ripe piece of fruit, a good glass of wine, a walk at dawn—and immerse yourself in sensory delight. Place full attention on the experience. Then, write a captured moment.

_____

_____

_____

_____

_____

_____

_____

_____

_____

_____

_____

_____

_____

_____

_____

_____

_____

_____

_____

_____

KEY #1: RESILIENCE. How have you managed challenges in the past several weeks?

WRITE ON! Check in with resilience skills and strategies. How are you falling down? How are you getting up? What are you learning?

_____

_____

_____

_____

_____

_____

_____

_____

_____

_____

_____

_____

_____

_____

_____

_____

_____

_____

_____

_____

_____

_____

_____

ESCAPE INTO A STORY WORLD. Reading fiction is a go-to touchstone for Dana. "I've always enjoyed escaping into a story world. It has a way of putting life into perspective and fosters empathy for characters who have it worse than me," she says.

WRITE ON! Do you lose yourself in a story world—fiction, film, television, video game? How does this escape help with life perspective?

_____

_____

_____

_____

_____

_____

_____

_____

_____

_____

_____

_____

_____

_____

_____

_____

_____

_____

_____

_____

_____

_____

_____

_____

MINDFUL EQUILIBRIUM. A third element of Dr. Neff's self-compassion approach is a willingness to observe negative emotions "with openness and clarity." She says it is important to "take a balanced approach to our negative emotions so that feelings are neither suppressed nor exaggerated."

WRITE ON! Write a story about a time you stuffed down or exploded a negative feeling. Write another story about a time you were able to compassionately intervene and mindfully manage a negative feeling. If you don't have such a story, make one up.

_____

_____

_____

_____

_____

WEEKLY REVIEW. Read over the week's entries, reflections, or both. How do you rank your anxiety this week? How do you rank your use of writing? How is the realistic progress of your intentions going? Are you noticing changes?

On a scale of 1 (low) to 7 (high), rate your week:

Anxiety?	①	②	③	④	⑤	⑥	⑦
Writing process?	①	②	③	④	⑤	⑥	⑦
Intentions?	①	②	③	④	⑤	⑥	⑦
Noticing shifts?	①	②	③	④	⑤	⑥	⑦

WRITE ON! Write observations as you rate your week. Note any connections you may see.

_____

_____

_____

_____

_____

SETTING INTENTION. What are three intentions this week that will advance your visions?

WRITE ON! Has your current reality moved closer to your vision in the last week? Every small intention you place attention and take action on closes the gap between current reality and vision.

_____

_____

_____

_____

_____

_____

_____

_____

MANTRAS. In his work on writing practice for process meditation, Dr. Progoff interprets Hindu/Buddhist traditions of mantras, or centering phrases, for the journal writer. He recommends using seven-syllable phrases: "the silent gift of the trees," "the yin and the yang aligning." Place verbs in gerund form (-ing): "river flowing to the sea," "breathing in and breathing out."

WRITE ON! Write seven-syllable mantras. Say them aloud, or under your breath, to find their rhythms, substituting words as needed. Note the one that feels most resonant and use it in your centering process.

_____

_____

_____

_____

_____

_____

DO NOT DISTURB. Trevor Haynes, author of a report on the neurotransmitter dopamine and smartphones, says that a barrage of pings and vibrations can be emotionally exhausting. The report recommends the phone's DO NOT DISTURB function, which puts you in control of when and where you receive messages and notifications.

WRITE ON! The report acknowledges that setting a phone to DND can itself be anxiety producing. Write about how it would feel to disable part of your notifications.

_____

_____

_____

_____

_____

_____

_____

_____

_____

_____

_____

_____

_____

_____

_____

_____

_____

_____

_____

_____

KEY #2: OUTLOOK. How is your outlook? Are you having better-feeling thoughts?

WRITE ON! Check in with yourself. Read back and reflect. Any patterns? Major takeaways?

_____

_____

_____

_____

_____

_____

_____

_____

_____

_____

_____

_____

_____

_____

_____

_____

_____

_____

_____

_____

_____

YELLOW ZONE AS ALLY. Dr. Hanson talks about the red zone of stress, the yellow transition zone, and the green zone of calm. The yellow zone is your ally. When you feel your body/mind moving into red, take action—breathe, relax, empty the dishwasher, reach out to connect, write. Do something small and simple to transition back to yellow, then to green.

WRITE ON! Write a simple mindfulness plan to move yourself to yellow the next time you hit the red zone. Write it on a Post-it Note or index card and keep it with you.

HYDRATION CHECK-IN. Are you remembering to drink at least eight small or six large glasses of water a day for healthy hydration?

WRITE ON! Take a moment to appreciate that, with tragic exceptions, there is an excellent chance that wherever you live in the United States, your tap water is drinkable. Write a thank-you letter or ode to water for being a life-giving and mood-enhancing elixir.

_____

_____

_____

_____

_____

WEEKLY REVIEW. Read over the week's entries, reflections, or both. How do you rank your anxiety this week? How do you rank your use of writing? How is the realistic progress of your intentions going? Are you noticing changes?

On a scale of 1 (low) to 7 (high), rate your week:

Anxiety?	①	②	③	④	⑤	⑥	⑦
Writing process?	①	②	③	④	⑤	⑥	⑦
Intentions?	①	②	③	④	⑤	⑥	⑦
Noticing shifts?	①	②	③	④	⑤	⑥	⑦

WRITE ON! Write observations as you rate your week. Note any connections you may see.

_____

_____

_____

_____

SETTING INTENTION. Keeping your weekly intentions in positive language helps with attention, the third key to well-being.

WRITE ON! What are three intentions for this week? Practice combining your intentions with attention this week.

_____

_____

_____

_____

_____

_____

_____

_____

_____

_____

_____

_____

_____

_____

_____

_____

_____

_____

_____

_____

_____

EVERYDAY NORMAL. This week and next, we will explore the "Pennebaker Paradigm," a series of four writing processes done sequentially with instructions to "write deeply about a stressful experience" in a structured way. This is the basic expressive writing research model, and it predictably results in physiological and emotional benefits. I have adapted it to include pre- and post-writing sets of "feeling" words, a reflection write, and a focus on "everyday normal" problems instead of stressful or traumatic topics. We will be writing the four parts of the Pennebaker Paradigm with my adaptations.

WRITE ON! Make a list of three or four "everyday normal" problems—stuff that is always going on, like the power struggle with your teen, dealings with your unreasonable boss, or the self-care that falls off the to-do list. Write a paragraph—no more—to frame each situation.

HAPPINESS HABIT #3: FORGIVENESS. In a 2001 study, participants were instructed to vividly imagine having empathy for someone who had harmed them. They also imagined actively forgiving the person. After, participants felt more in control of their thoughts and feelings. They felt less angry, sad, and stressed when they simply *thought* about forgiveness.

WRITE ON! Practice this with a minor character in your life that did little harm. You can either do this as a self-guided imagery, or you can write a letter. Write reflections after.

_____

_____

_____

_____

_____

_____

_____

_____

_____

KEY #3: ATTENTION. To what are you paying attention in recent weeks?

WRITE ON! Check in with yourself on your attention.

_____

_____

_____

_____

_____

_____

_____

_____

PENNEBAKER #1. Choose a story from your "everyday normal" list (Day 2). The entire process should take about 15 minutes. Write a list of "three feeling words" (Week 20, Day 2) at the start of each writing session and again at the end of the reflection write.

WRITE ON! Set your timer to 10 minutes. Breathe, and think about your chosen story. Write three feeling words. Then write the story of this everyday normal issue. Tell both facts and feelings, both content and affect. Tell the story any way you wish, but keep your pen moving; don't stop to edit or rewrite. At the end, read and reflect. Write three more feeling words.

_____

_____

_____

_____

_____

_____

_____

_____

_____

_____

_____

_____

_____

_____

_____

_____

_____

_____

_____

PENNEBAKER #2. Continue working with the same story. Again, you'll spend about 15 minutes total. Yesterday, you wrote the story of your chosen topic.

WRITE ON! Set the timer to 10 minutes. Breathe, and think about your chosen story. Write three feeling words. Then write more of the story of this everyday normal issue. This time, add in details, layers, and parts of the story that you forgot to tell. Don't stop to edit or rewrite. At the end, read and reflect. Write three more feeling words.

_____

_____

_____

_____

_____

_____

_____

_____

_____

_____

_____

_____

_____

_____

_____

_____

_____

_____

_____

_____

_____

WEEKLY REVIEW. Read over the week's entries, reflections, or both. How do you rank your anxiety this week? How do you rank your use of writing? How is the realistic progress of your intentions going? Are you noticing changes?

On a scale of 1 (low) to 7 (high), rate your week:

Anxiety?	①	②	③	④	⑤	⑥	⑦
Writing process?	①	②	③	④	⑤	⑥	⑦
Intentions?	①	②	③	④	⑤	⑥	⑦
Noticing shifts?	①	②	③	④	⑤	⑥	⑦

WRITE ON! Write observations as you rate your week. Note any connections you may see.

_____

_____

_____

_____

_____

_____

_____

_____

_____

_____

_____

_____

_____

_____

_____

_____

_____

SETTING INTENTION. What would you like to create this week? Keep them week-size.

WRITE ON! When you write three intentions, make sure they are specific and time-limited enough to see completion or significant progress in one week's time.

_____

_____

_____

_____

_____

_____

_____

PENNEBAKER #3. This week, we'll continue in the same pattern with the same story. Again, you'll spend about 20 minutes total and again you'll write three feeling words at the start of each writing session and at the end of the reflection write. In last week's second writing exercise, you told more of the story of your everyday normal issue, adding in details and layers.

WRITE ON! Again: 15 minutes, breathe, three feeling words. Today, we explore meaning. What is the impact or meaning of having this story as part of your life? What do you move toward or away from as a result of this story? Read, reflect, and write your three feeling words.

_____

_____

_____

_____

_____

_____

_____

_____

HAPPINESS HABIT #4: FLOW. The state of intense absorption in an activity or experience is inherently rewarding; we are suspended in a timeless pleasure that leaves us sated. Flow is not limited to creative activities. Indeed, any activity infused with mindfulness can trend toward flow.

WRITE ON! Naomi Shihab Nye's poem "Daily" perfectly describes flow in everyday life. Pay exquisite attention to your one singular ordinary life and write what you discover. Perhaps it will take the form of a list poem, as hers does.

_____

_____

_____

_____

_____

_____

_____

_____

KEY #4: GENEROSITY. How is your generosity of heart, mind, body, money, and service these last weeks? Who is being generous to you? Are you generous with yourself?

WRITE ON! Check in on your generosity experiences and takeaways from the last few weeks, and write about them.

_____

_____

_____

_____

_____

_____

_____

_____

PENNEBAKER #4. We'll follow the same pattern. This is the last write. In the previous one, you explored meaning and the impact of the problem.

WRITE ON! Center yourself with breath and write three feeling words. Today, we synthesize and look forward. What do you see freshly or differently? What might you keep, and what might you cut away? Has anything changed or shifted? You can be more thoughtful here, pausing to let ideas form, but keep writing for the full 10 minutes. At the end, read and reflect. Write three more feeling words.

_____

_____

_____

_____

_____

_____

_____

_____

_____

_____

_____

_____

_____

_____

_____

_____

_____

_____

FEELING-WORD SETS. On paper or screen, create a chart that has three rows and four columns. In the top row, label the columns Day 1, Day , 2, Day 3, and Day 4. Enter your feeling-word sets (the ones you wrote before and after each of the four writing processes) in the top and bottom rows for each day. Then compare, top to bottom and left to right. Also compare your first set of words (Day 1, top) to your last set of words (Day 4, bottom). Write about what you notice.

WRITE ON! Do your feeling-word sets tell a story? Write it. Or, write your observations and reflections.

_____

_____

_____

_____

_____

WEEKLY REVIEW. Read over the week's entries, reflections, or both. How do you rank your anxiety this week? How do you rank your use of writing? How is the realistic progress of your intentions going? Are you noticing changes?

On a scale of 1 (low) to 7 (high), rate your week:

Anxiety?	1	2	3	4	5	6	7
Writing process?	1	2	3	4	5	6	7
Intentions?	1	2	3	4	5	6	7
Noticing shifts?	1	2	3	4	5	6	7

WRITE ON! Write observations as you rate your week. Note any connections you may see.

_____

_____

_____

_____

SETTING INTENTION. It's Intentions Day!

WRITE ON! What are three intentions for this week? How did you do last week?

_____

_____

_____

_____

_____

_____

_____

_____

INNER WISDOM. Dr. Progoff's inner wisdom journal process allows you to tune into the "still, small voice" that all spiritual traditions urge us toward. Metaphors, symbols, and archetypes often show up.

WRITE ON! Quiet your mind, form a question, repeat your mantra (Week 45, Day 2) and sit in mindful silence until you are inspired to write. Accept what comes. Continue until you feel complete, or until your designated time is reached. Read and reflect.

_____

_____

_____

_____

_____

_____

_____

_____

HAPPINESS HABIT #5: POST-TRAUMATIC GROWTH. Friedrich Nietzsche said, "That which does not kill us makes us stronger" (a sentiment pop singer Kelly Clarkson echoed). Post-traumatic growth is a new science of encouraging transformation from life's most difficult circumstances by finding meaning and purpose in the hardship.

WRITE ON! Think back to a past hardship or difficulty. How are you stronger as a result? What meaning did you find that still serves you? Write out the story.

_____

_____

_____

_____

_____

_____

_____

_____

_____

_____

_____

_____

_____

_____

_____

_____

_____

_____

_____

_____

KEY #1: RESILIENCE. How have you managed challenges in the past several weeks?

WRITE ON! Check in with resilience skills and strategies. How are you falling down? How are you getting up? What are you learning?

_____

_____

_____

_____

_____

_____

_____

_____

_____

_____

_____

_____

_____

_____

_____

_____

_____

_____

_____

_____

_____

_____

_____

_____

HOPE AS PREDICTOR. In a study reported in *Behavior Therapy,* clinical psychologist Matthew Gallagher of the University of Houston finds that hope is a trait that becomes "a strong predictor" of recovery from anxiety disorders.

WRITE ON! As we turn toward closure with this journal process, how is your state of hope? Do you have confidence you can continue the process you have begun and deepened? What do you need?

_____

_____

_____

_____

_____

_____

_____

_____

_____

_____

_____

_____

_____

_____

_____

_____

_____

_____

TOUCHBACK: TOOLS. You've gained many toolkits in this inquiry: anxiety management strategies, mindfulness strategies, four keys to well-being, loads of journaling techniques/prompts/resources, cognitive-behavioral strategies and tools, breathwork, nutrition, hydration, science, intention-setting, reflection, and more.

WRITE ON! Customize your own action plan going forward. What will you remember and use?

_____

_____

_____

_____

_____

_____

WEEKLY REVIEW. Read over the week's entries, reflections, or both. How do you rank your anxiety this week? How do you rank your use of writing? How is the realistic progress of your intentions going? Are you noticing changes?

On a scale of 1 (low) to 7 (high), rate your week:

Anxiety?	①	②	③	④	⑤	⑥	⑦
Writing process?	①	②	③	④	⑤	⑥	⑦
Intentions?	①	②	③	④	⑤	⑥	⑦
Noticing shifts?	①	②	③	④	⑤	⑥	⑦

WRITE ON! Write observations as you rate your week. Note any connections you may see.

_____

_____

_____

_____

_____

SETTING INTENTION. The weekly process of setting intentions brings focus and action orientation to your days. Be sure that your intentions are framed in positive language. Specify what you want rather than what you want to avoid.

WRITE ON! What are three intentions for this week? These can be related to any area of your life. Break larger intentions into week-size bites.

_____

_____

_____

_____

_____

_____

SILENCE. Sometimes we come to a pause, a full stop, a draining of will. It can feel like not caring, or giving up. Maybe it's assimilation, when something is happening while it looks like nothing is happening. William Stafford's poem "Ask Me," about a hidden current in a frozen river, describes assimilation.

WRITE ON! Write a story about a time when you felt mute. Write another story about a time when your silence was part of a process that only made sense in retrospect.

_____

_____

_____

_____

_____

_____

_____

_____

POETRY. Journal poetry is whatever you want it to be. Some people write poems right in their journals. Others play with words in the journal, moving a poem through lots of drafts. Some write a journal entry and break the lines in interesting places, giving it the look and feel and rhythm of a poem. You can start with a line or image from a favorite poem or poet. Title a poem with the first story in your news feed. Write an alphapoem using the whole alphabet, A–Z. You can also use a word or phrase written vertically down the page. Have fun!

WRITE ON! Today, write any sort of poem in your journal.

KEY #2: OUTLOOK. How is your outlook? Are you finding yourself more able to assume positive intent? Looking at the possible good in a challenge? Having better-feeling thoughts?

WRITE ON! Check in with yourself. Read back and reflect. Any patterns? Major takeaways?

PRACTICING THE KEYS. A year of consistent focus on the four keys to well-being—resilience, outlook, attention, and generosity—has given your neural circuitry a good chance to fire and wire around health-affirming thoughts and behaviors.

WRITE ON! How can you continue to be consistent with the four keys? You may want to continue weekly check-in reviews, as you've done in this journal. Consider your options.

_____

_____

_____

_____

_____

_____

_____

_____

_____

_____

_____

_____

_____

_____

_____

_____

_____

_____

_____

_____

_____

_____

JOURNAL CONTINUATION. Let's make a plan for your journal continuation. It's not necessary to write every day, although it's fine if you do. (Be self-compassionate if you miss days.) Shoot for somewhere between once a week (to check in, review the week, set intentions) and three or four times a week (to stay current, process material, note progress, and deepen). You can also keep a notebook in your bag or backpack and write five-minute sprints whenever you want to capture a quick thought, feeling, or experience.

WRITE ON! What feels like the best journal plan going forward? Listen to your gut.

_____

_____

_____

_____

_____

_____

WEEKLY REVIEW. Read over the week's entries, reflections, or both. How do you rank your anxiety this week? How do you rank your use of writing? How is the realistic progress of your intentions going? Are you noticing changes?

On a scale of 1 (low) to 7 (high), rate your week:

Anxiety?	①	②	③	④	⑤	⑥	⑦
Writing process?	①	②	③	④	⑤	⑥	⑦
Intentions?	①	②	③	④	⑤	⑥	⑦
Noticing shifts?	①	②	③	④	⑤	⑥	⑦

WRITE ON! Write observations as you rate your week. Note any connections you may see.

_____

_____

_____

_____

SETTING INTENTION. It's time to write intentions!

WRITE ON! What are three intentions for this week?

_____

_____

_____

_____

_____

_____

_____

_____

A GOODBYE LETTER. We are coming to the end of a journey that lasted a year or more. You've covered a lot of ground, written miles of words. You're a lot different than when you started! Think back to who you were then, and who you are now.

WRITE ON! Write a goodbye letter to the "you" that started this program. You have companioned yourself beautifully through this journey. Give a written standing ovation to that brave you who got here, however long it took, day by day.

_____

_____

_____

_____

_____

_____

_____

_____

HAPPINESS HABIT #6: CELEBRATE GOOD NEWS. Sharing successes with others, whether the success is yours or theirs, enriches all. Researchers say that passing on congratulations and relishing the occasion lead to soaking up the moment. And don't overlook yourself: Take pride in your success and let people celebrate *you*.

WRITE ON! Recall a time when you were at a festive celebration, for yourself or someone else. Rekindle that fire and savor the experience. Write about it using juicy verbs and lavish adjectives.

KEY #3: ATTENTION. To what or whom are you paying attention in recent weeks?

WRITE ON! Check in with yourself on your attention.

_____

_____

_____

_____

_____

_____

_____

_____

_____

_____

_____

_____

_____

_____

_____

_____

_____

_____

_____

_____

_____

_____

_____

_____

IF YOU FALTER. Although it's nice to have freedom again after an intensive focus—who doesn't love summer vacations?—it can also leave us feeling a little wobbly. If you start to slip, have a rescue kit handy. What are five things you know will reliably work for you if you feel like you're losing ground?

WRITE ON! Write out your rescue kit. What specific tools, techniques, or strategies will you enact immediately if you falter?

_____

_____

_____

_____

_____

_____

_____

_____

_____

_____

_____

_____

_____

_____

_____

_____

_____

_____

_____

_____

_____

TOUCHBACK: INNER ALLY, SUPERPOWER, SAFE PLACE. In meditation, take yourself to your safe place, where you meet your inner ally for lunch and a chat. Play out a guided visualization in which you and your inner ally bring your superpowers into play to help map out a strategy for this transition. Ask for a symbol that will serve as a touchstone.

WRITE ON! Write down your observations of the visualization. What was your symbol? What does it mean to you?

_____

_____

_____

_____

_____

WEEKLY REVIEW. Read over the week's entries, reflections, or both. How do you rank your anxiety this week? How do you rank your use of writing? How is the realistic progress of your intentions going? Are you noticing changes?

On a scale of 1 (low) to 7 (high), rate your week:

Anxiety?	①	②	③	④	⑤	⑥	⑦
Writing process?	①	②	③	④	⑤	⑥	⑦
Intentions?	①	②	③	④	⑤	⑥	⑦
Noticing shifts?	①	②	③	④	⑤	⑥	⑦

WRITE ON! Write observations as you rate your week. Note any connections you see.

_____

_____

_____

_____

_____

SETTING INTENTION. What has progressed or manifested as a result of your intentions?

WRITE ON! Reflect on your progress and write three intentions for this week.

_____

_____

_____

_____

_____

_____

_____

LOOKING FORWARD: WHAT DO YOU WANT TO REMEMBER? Imagine yourself one year from today (your name will be MePlus1). You're one year more skilled at managing anxiety through mindfulness and writing. You've got a mindfulness pantry stuffed with ways of thinking, behaving, feeling, and believing. You're deepening habits and behaviors. You're more practiced at better-feeling thoughts.

WRITE ON! Write a "welcome to your future" letter to your today self, from MePlus1. What tools and resources will have gotten you through the next year? What does MePlus1 want you to remember? What advice does MePlus1 offer?

_____

_____

_____

_____

_____

_____

_____

_____

HAPPINESS HABIT #7: SEEK OUT THE BITTERSWEET. Bittersweet experiences are a mix of two opposing emotions, often happiness and sadness, and typically involve a transitory experience, such as a trip or promotion or graduation. The edge of sadness creates an urgency to appreciate the good.

WRITE ON! Write about a bittersweet experience, perhaps the ending of this journal. What will you miss? What is the good you will savor?

_____

_____

_____

_____

_____

_____

_____

_____

_____

_____

_____

_____

_____

_____

_____

_____

_____

_____

_____

_____

_____

_____

KEY #4: GENEROSITY. How is your generosity of heart, mind, body, money, and service these last weeks? Who is being generous to you? Are you generous with yourself?

WRITE ON! Check in on your experiences with generosity and takeaways the last few weeks.

_____

_____

_____

_____

_____

_____

_____

_____

_____

_____

_____

_____

_____

_____

_____

_____

_____

_____

_____

_____

_____

_____

_____

A LETTER TO ANXIETY. Your relationship with anxiety has likely changed since you began this journal. Anxiety may continue to companion you, but it's possible the relationship can be more of a partnership from here.

WRITE ON! Write a letter to anxiety acknowledging the shift in your relationship. Invite anxiety into a new partnership, and suggest what that might mean. Anxiety may want to write a letter back!

_____

_____

_____

_____

_____

_____

_____

_____

_____

_____

_____

_____

_____

_____

_____

_____

_____

_____

_____

_____

ONE-YEAR INTENTIONS. We have been working in weekly units of intention-setting. You can also gaze at a horizon far in the future, such as one year or five years. Think about what you deeply want for yourself going forward. Write five to seven intentions you have for the next year. What do you want to do, be, and have?

WRITE ON! Write your intentions for the next year. If you could make significant progress toward achieving some or all of these intentions, how would your life be different and better?

_____

_____

_____

_____

_____

_____

WEEKLY REVIEW. Read over the week's entries, reflections, or both. How do you rank your anxiety this week? How do you rank your use of writing? How is the realistic progress of your intentions going? Are you noticing changes?

On a scale of 1 (low) to 7 (high), rate your week:

Anxiety?	①	②	③	④	⑤	⑥	⑦
Writing process?	①	②	③	④	⑤	⑥	⑦
Intentions?	①	②	③	④	⑤	⑥	⑦
Noticing shifts?	①	②	③	④	⑤	⑥	⑦

WRITE ON! Write observations as you rate your week. Note any connections you may see.

_____

_____

_____

_____

INTENTIONS IN REVIEW. All year, you've set intentions for your week. You've worked on breaking big goals or intentions into week-size bites. You've tracked outcomes.

WRITE ON! Did the weekly intentions help you frame goals and tasks for the week? Did you usually meet your intentions?

_____

_____

_____

_____

_____

_____

_____

_____

_____

WRITING IN REVIEW. You've written your way through a whole year with focused attention. You've learned writing techniques and strategies, and you've written about your cognitive and emotional patterns. You've practiced mindful writing.

WRITE ON! What are the writing practices you will take from this experience?

_____

_____

_____

_____

_____

_____

_____

SCIENCE IN REVIEW. This year, you have learned about cognitive-behavioral therapy, neuroplasticity principles through Davidson's keys to well-being, the importance of healthy habits, the science of happiness, and more.

WRITE ON! What did you learn that was new? What knowledge did you refresh or extend? Is there anything you want to study more deeply?

_____

_____

_____

_____

_____

_____

_____

_____

_____

_____

_____

_____

_____

_____

_____

_____

_____

_____

_____

_____

_____

_____

THE FOUR KEYS IN REVIEW. You have spent a year exploring the four keys to well-being. You have practiced resilience, outlook, attention, and generosity every month for a year.

WRITE ON! How have you shifted in the four keys? Where are you noticing growth or change?

MINDFULNESS IN REVIEW. You've learned mindfulness tools, woven throughout the writing and daily doing. You've learned about breathwork, metaphors, attention, quieting the mind, and gently redirecting thoughts.

WRITE ON! Which mindfulness strategies are most useful for you? Write about any practices (e.g., writing, breathwork, sitting meditation, movement meditation) you are developing.

_____

_____

_____

_____

_____

_____

_____

_____

_____

_____

_____

_____

_____

_____

_____

_____

_____

_____

_____

_____

_____

_____

_____

WEEKLY REVIEWS. How have the weekly reviews served you as observational and tracking systems?

WRITE ON! If you like charts and graphs, you can make your own tracking documents and keep your own data.

_____

_____

_____

_____

_____

_____

_____

GRADUATION REVIEW. Overall, how would you rank yourself in the entire start-to-finish process?

On a scale of 1 (low) to 7 (high), rate your ending point:

Anxiety?	①	②	③	④	⑤	⑥	⑦
Writing process?	①	②	③	④	⑤	⑥	⑦
Intentions?	①	②	③	④	⑤	⑥	⑦
Noticing shifts?	①	②	③	④	⑤	⑥	⑦

WRITE ON! Share any last thoughts you may have about the process.

_____

_____

_____

_____

_____

_____

CONGRATULATIONS! YOU DID IT! You have come to the end of the journal. You are a champion!

Today, make yourself a graduation certificate. Make it as dazzling as you like. Or make yourself a collage or other piece of art as commemoration of your journey. Hang it up somewhere. You've earned it!

WRITE ON! Who are you becoming?

_____

_____

_____

_____

_____

_____

_____

_____

_____

_____

_____

_____

_____

_____

_____

_____

_____

_____

_____

_____

Acknowledgments

I AM GRATEFUL TO—

My manuscript readers, educational design expert Susie Phillips, self-directed neuroplasticity expert Deborah Ross, and change management expert Ken Perreault, whose invaluable feedback shaped the content and form of this book.

My large, lively, and always loving family, particularly my sister Cindy Oury, for her endless optimism and support.

The love of my life, Ken Perreault, who made sure I was fed, hydrated, and hugged during the last intense weeks of writing.

The nearly 200 survey participants who generously shared their own anxiety-management strategies.

My psychotherapy clients across 35 years whose struggles with anxiety disorders have deepened my compassion, educated me, and informed my treatment methods and writing prompts.

The worldwide journal therapy community—trainees, graduates, students, and writers in many languages and cultures.

The astonishing team at Sterling Publishing—my editor, Adam O'Brien; executive editor Barbara Berger, who invited me into this project; and everyone in graphic design, production, and sales. The combination is this author's dream team.

You, the reader of this book, for your courage and commitment. May writing be a bridge to your enhanced well-being.

Sources

Gratitude is offered to the following authors, researchers, and colleagues whose works are referenced in these pages.

CHRISTINA BALDWIN is an author and pioneer in the journal writing movement. She is the author of the book *The Seven Whispers,* among others.

AARON BECK, MD, is a psychiatrist and author who founded cognitive-behavioral therapy.

HERBERT BENSON, MD, is a cardiologist and founder of the Mind-Body Medical Institute at Massachusetts General Hospital. He created the Relaxation Response.

EDMUND BOURNE, PhD, is a clinical psychologist specializing in anxiety disorders. He is the author of the book *The Anxiety & Phobia Workbook,* among others.

NICKY CASE is a Canadian video game designer, whose creations include the open-source game *Adventures with Anxiety.*

RICHARD J. DAVIDSON, PhD, is a psychologist and neuroscientist who created the Center for Healthy Minds at the University of Wisconsin–Madison.

ALBERT ELLIS, PhD, (d. 2007) was a psychologist and author who founded the Rational Emotive Behavior Therapy (REBT) model.

MATTHEW GALLAGHER, PhD, is a psychologist specializing in positive psychology in the treatment of anxiety and PTSD.

RICK HANSON, PhD, is a psychologist and senior fellow at the Greater Good Science Center at UC Berkeley. He is the author of the book *Just One Thing,* among others.

SUSAN HANSTED, MFT, is a licensed marriage and family therapist and the founder of the Institute for Possibility Thinking.

TREVOR HAYNES is a contributing writer to *Science in the News,* a Harvard publication.

BURGHILD NINA HOLZER is a native Austrian who lives, writes and teaches in California. She is the author of the book *A Walk Between Heaven and Earth.*

WILLIAM JAMES was a nineteenth-century philosopher and psychologist who is considered to be one of the founding fathers of American psychology.

JON KABAT-ZINN, PhD, is a psychologist and the founding director of the Stress Reduction Clinic at the University of Massachusetts Medical School. He is the best-selling author of the book *Wherever You Go There You Are,* among others.

SONJA LYUBOMIRSKY, PhD, is a social psychologist and author of *The How of Happiness.*

LINDA TRICHTER METCALF, PhD, is the creator of the Proprioceptive Writing Method, which combines the art of literary criticism with therapeutic techniques. She is the co-author of the book *Writing the Mind Alive.*

UMA NAIDOO, MD, is a psychiatrist and professional chef who studies the relationship between food and mental health.

KRISTEN NEFF, PhD, is an educational psychologist who is pioneering the field of self-compassion. She is the author of *Self-Compassion.*

JAMES PENNEBAKER, PhD, is a research psychologist who pioneered evidence-based research in expressive writing and health. He is the author of the book *Writing to Heal,* among others.

IRA PROGOFF, PhD, (d. 1998) was a depth psychologist and the founder of the Intensive Journal method. He is the author of the book *At a Journal Workshop,* among others.

DEBORAH ROSS, LPC, is a licensed psychotherapist, certified journal therapist, and creator of the Your Brain on Ink method of self-directed neuroplasticity. She is the author of *Your Brain on Ink.*

ETI BEN-SIMON, PhD, is a psychologist at UC Berkeley, with a specialty in neuroscience.

TOBIN SIMON, PhD, is a poet and educator. He contributed to the development of the Propriceptive Writing Method and is the co-author of the book *Writing the Mind Alive.*

THÍCH THÔNG TRIÊT is a Zen Master and the creator of the Sunyata meditation method.

MATTHEW WALKER, PhD, is a psychologist and neuroscience professor at UC Berkeley who specializes in sleep research.

ABOUT THE AUTHOR

KATHLEEN (KAY) ADAMS LPC, PTR, is a best-selling author, speaker, psychotherapist, registered poetry/journal therapist, and visionary. Her first book, *Journal to the Self*, is a classic that helped define the field of journal therapy more than 30 years ago. She has further defined it in 12 more books.

Kay is a beloved teacher whose innovative work has helped hundreds of thousands of people heal, change, and grow. She is the voice of journal therapy at conferences, hospitals, mental health agencies, and seminars around the world.

A tireless advocate for the healing power of writing, Kay is a three-time recipient of the National Association for Poetry Therapy's Distinguished Service Award. In 2015, the Center for Journal Therapy received NAPT's Education Award for its leadership and excellence in education and training. Kay has also received awards for her work bringing journal therapy to populations as diverse as people with HIV/AIDS, breast cancer survivors, recovering addicts, and survivors of violent crime.

In 2008, after years of training in small groups or guided independent study, Kay launched the Therapeutic Writing Institute (TWI), a fully online credentials training program for both therapists and community facilitators. TWI is internationally acknowledged to be the premier source of education and training in therapeutic writing.

In 2018 Kay added a second online school, Journalversity, for personal journal writers and psychotherapists seeking continuing education in journal therapy.

In an internet poll, Kathleen Adams was listed (with Anne Frank and Anaïs Nin) as one of the three most significant influences on contemporary journal keeping.

Journal Therapy for Calming Anxiety is her thirteenth book.

See more at www.journaltherapy.com.